Life is like that sometimes

Also by Khaya Dlanga

It's The Answers For Me (2021)

'This is a glimpse into South Africa, a glimpse into humanity: our loves, fears, desires and traumas … so well put together.'
– Thuso Mbedu

These Things Really Do Happen To Me (2018)
Shortlisted for the 2019 SA Book Awards – Adult Non-Fiction

'Imagine the most fascinating stories your best friend ever told you. This is a book full of them!'
– Trevor Noah

To Quote Myself: A Memoir (2016, 2015)
Shortlisted for the 2015 Sunday Times Non-Fiction Prize

'Stories like Dlanga's are important. They prove to young people that the conditions under which they are born should not determine who they end up being. The world is littered with people who started from zero or even a minus, but made it. Unfortunately, they are in the minority. *To Quote Myself* is also a deceptive motivational tool, because it's a serious life lesson that's couched in humour …'
– *City Press Voices*

In My Arrogant Opinion (2012)

'This is just one in a series of entertaining pocket books, aptly called THE YOUNGSTERS. The youth-aimed series features prominent young South African personalities and tackles issues that range from the cultural and political, right down to hair weaves and clubbing etiquette.'
– *Business Day Wanted*

Life is like that sometimes

KHAYA DLANGA

MACMILLAN

First published in 2025
by Pan Macmillan South Africa
Private Bag X19
Northlands
Johannesburg
2116

www.panmacmillan.co.za

ISBN 978-1-77010-858-5
e-ISBN 978-1-77010-857-8

© 2025 Khaya Dlanga

All rights reserved. No part of this publication may be reproduced, stored in or introduced into a retrieval system, or transmitted, in any form or by any means (electronic, mechanical, photocopying, recording or otherwise), without the prior written permission of the publisher. Any person who does any unauthorised act in relation to this publication may be liable to criminal prosecution and civil claims for damages.

Editing by Kelly Norwood-Young
Proofreading by Jane Bowman
Design and typesetting by Nyx Design
Cover design by Ayanda Phasha

In memory of my mother, Nonceba Dlanga,
and my brother, Nganga Dlanga. Your love outlives you –
it is a fire that warms me on the coldest nights and
a light that guides me through the darkest days.

Author's note

Life is like that sometimes is a journey through nostalgia, loss, and the bittersweetness of life. It revisits my childhood in Dutyini, a time filled with the vivid memories of growing up in rural Transkei. But as much as it captures those simpler days, this book also delves into the profound weight of loss – the ache that lingers when those we love are no longer here.

Loss is universal, but it's never simple. No matter how much we know it's an inevitable part of life, nothing prepares us for the void it leaves or the tiny, unexpected moments that catch us off guard and break our hearts all over again. Yet, amid this grief, life insists on moving forward, teaching us to find meaning in the pain and joy of the memories.

For some readers, a chapter or two may feel familiar, echoing parts of my earlier books. Don't be alarmed nor dismayed. In those past works, certain stories were briefly mentioned in just a sentence or two – enough to spark curiosity but not satisfy it. Over the years, readers have told me how much they wished I'd shared those stories in full. So, here they are, expanded and given the space they deserve.

The stories in this book, while deeply personal, are also

reflections of the lives of millions of South Africans – their resilience, humour, heartbreak, and hope. The only difference is that I have been afforded the privilege of writing them down, of preserving moments that many others quietly live through without the chance to share them with the world. This is both a responsibility and gift I accept and hope to use with humility and grace.

Before I close, I want to address a subject that feels urgent but often unspoken: the disparity in book-buying, publishing, and reading patterns within South Africa.

White South Africans remain the largest book buyers in the country, a pattern rooted in the economic and historical inequalities that still shape our society today. Yet, within this group of avid book buyers, books by black writers are purchased in significantly smaller numbers than those by white authors. This imbalance reflects both historical and systemic barriers.

Economic disparities play a significant role, with black South Africans earning an average of just thirteen cents for every rand earned by their white counterparts, according to Standard Bank.[1] These realities make it more difficult for many black South Africans to afford books, limiting access to stories, including those by black authors.

At the same time, structural inequities in publishing exacerbate the issue. Between 2019 and 2021, white authors made up 58% of published fiction writers, compared to 31% for black writers and 11% for other people of colour, according to the *Mail & Guardian*.[2] Fewer opportunities for black writers to be published mean that their stories often struggle to gain visibility.

Compounding these challenges is the limited engagement

with black-authored stories among white readers, who remain the largest segment of book buyers. Together, these factors contribute to a landscape where black stories – though rich in their breadth and depth – often fail to reach the audiences they deserve across all demographics.

This raises a difficult but necessary question: Are we, as a nation, doing enough to ensure that black stories are seen, heard, and valued by all South Africans?

Stories have the unique power to connect us. They allow us to step into each other's shoes, to walk paths we might not otherwise tread, and to see the world through each other's eyes. To bridge the chasms left by history and circumstance, we must embrace the richness of all our voices.

While black readers frequently engage with books by both black and white authors, I urge white book buyers to do the same: to actively seek out, support, and engage with the stories of black South Africans. If you are already doing this, I thank you. I encourage you to share these stories with your friends, family, and book clubs. Together, we can ensure that all voices are heard, valued, and celebrated.

A country that reads across its divides can grow beyond them.

As a final note, I hope this book reminds you that you are not alone in your joys or your sorrows. Life, as messy and unpredictable as it is, has a way of weaving beauty and meaning into even the hardest moments. And perhaps, as you read, you'll find a piece of your own story within these pages.

The man in past tense

I only realised that I had been at my father's funeral in Danti village (or, as others liked to call it, Jojo) almost two years later. I was seven, going on eight years old, when it finally occurred to me why my little sister, Siki Dlanga, my mother, Nonceba Dlanga, and I had sat at the front of the church with a coffin in front of us shortly after my sixth birthday. The realisation came slowly, as if I stumbled upon puzzle pieces one at a time.

The funeral had taken place about two weeks after the extravagant birthday celebrations my mother had arranged for my birthday in Dutyini – celebrations held without my father, who was presumed to be alive and working in Johannesburg at the time. In fact, he was already dead; we just didn't know it yet.

My father's passing and funeral slipped by me as unnoticed as a whisper into the wind. Nobody told me that my father had died – at least not while I was awake.

There is a belief among some South African cultures that pre-adolescent children shouldn't be told directly when someone close to them has died, especially a parent. It's thought that a child would find it too traumatic to bear or understand the finality of death. Instead, someone appointed by the family waits until the child is in deep sleep and whispers the news into their ear. The hope is that the subconscious will take in the information gently, like placing a sleeping child to bed.

But there is nothing gentle about death. It reaches harshly, with no kindness, leaving the living in a state of turmoil and emotional paralysis.

On my birthday, I was playing in the yard with my cousins when I heard the wailing of the grown-ups coming from the hut where they were huddled together after receiving the news via telegram.

Of course, no one told us what had happened, but we all noticed the sudden change in the adults' mood. The celebratory atmosphere had vanished, replaced by a heavy, hurried and burdened energy. Clothes were packed hastily, and the joyful, noisy playing came to an abrupt end. We were quickly bundled into a car and driven all the way to Danti, my father's home.

There, I simply went where I was told, wore the clothes I was given, and enjoyed the excessive attention I received from unfamiliar relatives who somehow knew my sister and me. Adults seemed to have an extraordinary expectation that you should remember them.

I don't think I ever asked about him that first year after he died because I hardly knew him. He had gone to work in Johannesburg when Siki and I were very young, so it never occurred to me to ask after him. Siki was still only three years old, with her fourth birthday four months away when he passed away.

My childhood was a constant boom of activity at my grandparents' home, too lively for me to have any existential crisis about a father I barely remembered. The house was always bustling with human traffic. Relatives were always expected and were a welcome interruption. There was none of today's modern etiquette of announcing visits in advance – visitors simply showed up, and there was no surprise when they did. If anything, an unexpected and unwelcome surprise would be a day without any visitors at all.

I had many duties as a young boy. I helped Makhulu, my grandmother, Vuywelwa Victoria Boyce, feed her chickens in the mornings and brought out dishes filled with food for our many dogs.

Her isiXhosa title, Makhulu, carried the warmth of generations, a word that meant more than 'Grandmother'; it echoed the matriarchal strength that anchored generations of Xhosa families.

I'd open the gate to let the geese out, and throughout the day, relatives and neighbours would call my name from the gate so I could let them in, as they feared our dogs.

By midday, when the sun floated high overhead with no wind, visitors slowed down, except for those with serious business to discuss with my grandparents. It was mostly my grandmother who received the bulk of these visitors. I especially enjoyed the more 'important' visitors. They would sit with my grandmother on grass mats on the veranda, or in the lounge if it was too hot. A relative living with us would make tea, and I'd often be asked to take the tray out to them.

Sometimes, Makhulu would make me sit behind her and pour me tea on a saucer. I'd slurp the toffee-coloured tea with pure joy, as nothing better could happen to me that day. It was always Joko tea mixed with the day's fresh cow milk that I had helped milk. Once I was done with the tea, I would take the tray back to the kitchen, sneaking a teaspoon of sugar along the way. Sugar was like gold in Dutyini; it was stored under lock and key, and the only sugar out was for tea or porridge in the morning. I'd heard of children who received hidings for being caught stealing sugar.

Many of our neighbours were cousins, and those my age were my friends. Their fathers were also absent, working in Johannesburg's mines or on Durban's sugarcane farms. So there was nothing particularly unique about my father not being around. In fact, I saw my grandfather daily, while many of my friends didn't have the good fortune of having any father figure like this at home. My grandfather, Alfred Kaiser Boyce, was the de facto elder in our community.

My uncle, Senzangakhona Mshumi, who had married my mother's sister, Nolulama, also visited often – far more frequently than many fathers did, which made the absence of my own father less noticeable.

I worked out that my father had died the way you solve a puzzle. When adults talked to me about this man, Zandisile, they always spoke in the past tense. It didn't register with me right away, but I gradually pieced it together. They spoke of his acts of valour, how he was a courageous man who once fought boys from a neighbouring village singlehandedly in a stick fight.

One story that has always stayed with me is about my father during his time as a traffic officer in the then Transkei in the early 1980s. One day, he was unceremoniously summoned by his superiors to Mthatha, at the traffic department head offices. When he arrived, he was ushered into an office where several of them were waiting, visibly unhappy.

They presented him with a file – a record of all the fines he had issued. The question they posed was pointed: why did he only seem to fine white drivers? And not just for significant violations – he fined them for the smallest of infringements too.

My father's response was that most of the cars on the road were driven by white people, but his superiors were unsatisfied by his response. He was given a formal warning and sent on his way.

They may have suspected something was amiss, but they did not know the truth behind his actions. My father's own father, my grandfather, Thambile Paulos Dlanga, had been forced out of Lesotho, where he had been exiled. He was captured and tortured until he was partially paralysed. He suffered multiple strokes and eventually died. My father, who was barely a teenager when his father passed away, carried that pain every single day.

My father's actions were not just the strict enforcement of traffic laws – in his own quiet but deliberate way, they became a form of personal protest against a system that had stolen his father from him.

That quiet defiance, though rarely spoken about, was something that defined him in so many ways. Adults talking about my father would describe him not only as courageous but also as a generous man with a kindly smile and a slight lisp. They always said how much I looked like him, this man I barely knew. When his name came up, a sense of nostalgia always accompanied it. Every. Single. Time.

Bit by bit, I put these puzzle pieces together and realised this man they spoke of in the past tense, with such a wistful look in their eyes, was gone. There was no formal announcement – just a quiet knowing, as if by osmosis, that settled in me over time.

The *past-tense* man used to be my father. He *was* my father.

The wife-beater trial

Tat'omkhulu – my grandfather, Alfred Kaiser Boyce – had always played a father figure to me even when my father was still alive. I knew him far more than I did Zandisile, my father. He was the man whose example was always before me and someone I aspired to emulate.

His word carried weight, not just with me, but with anyone who had the privilege, or the misfortune of crossing his path. His name commanded respect and authority, and he never abused his position, despite being both feared and revered. Whatever he said was final and when he wanted to emphasise his words, he would often say, 'Lithi igama lam,' which translates to 'My word says.' It was his version of 'I have spoken.'

There was a security and assuredness in myself that I am certain came directly from knowing that I had him as a grandfather. It gave me a fearlessness and confidence in myself that felt unwarranted.

In many ways, it was fitting that his name was Kaiser, as he practically ruled the village, even though he was not the chief. My grandfather believed in protocol and had a deep respect for the chief, yet many matters were brought to him. I suspect that this was partly because the Boyce and Snama clan was a large part of the village.

As the head of the extended Boyce and Snama clan in the village, no family function or decision occurred without consulting him first. All Boyces carried the Snama clan name, but not all Snamas were Boyces. He was the head of all of them.

What truly cemented his power and influence, however, was his control over the village's cattle – the ultimate currency of rural life. He was the keeper of the cattle ledger, if you will, meticulously recording every transaction or event involving cattle. Whether a cow was bought, sold, lost, slaughtered, or if a calf was born, it all had to be reported to him. If a cow was sick and died without him having been informed of the cow's illness beforehand, there would be hell to pay when its death was eventually reported. He always had various medications on hand and administered injections to treat sickly cows. Every family's cattle records ran through him, making the entire village reliant on his knowledge and integrity.

When a member of the Snama clan came to complain that her husband was physically abusive, my grandfather convened imbizo for ityala (trial) at our family home. These types of family disagreement cases were held at our homestead next to the kraal under the old tractor shed made from zinc.

My mother had bought a tractor to plough fields in the village for cash, with my grandfather managing it, but over the years the unserviced tractor fell into disrepair and the business venture died a slow painful death. The tractor shed became my grandfather's place to sit during hot, sunny days.

The children were never allowed to be part of the hearings, but we always found ways to eavesdrop. The best way to catch snippets of what was happening was to get yourself called upon to deliver a small bucket of amarhewu from the kitchen mid-hearing. Amarhewu was always a welcome reprieve from the dry summer heat.

Naturally, this led to scrambles and squabbles among us for the honour of carrying the bucket. The winner would rush back, puffed up with pride, eager to spill the secrets of whatever they'd managed to overhear.

Most of the time, I was too young to fully understand the intricacies of the discussions. But between whispered retellings and wild speculation, we'd piece together the gist of what was going on.

As always, my grandfather sat on his special stool, which no one else was allowed to use. It was a simple tree stump, sturdy enough for a large man, and lower than the average modern-day chair. Everyone else sat in a V formation around him, with him at the apex. Anyone wishing to speak would stand to add weight (or lack thereof) to their argument. My grandfather listened attentively, occasionally interjecting with questions. Once everyone who had something to add was done, he would summarise the points made by both sides and ensure that each party agreed with how he'd represented their arguments before delivering his verdict.

One of the most famous cases he presided over involved physical abuse, and the sentence he handed down became the stuff of legend. A relative's wife accused him of beating her. The man had even struck her with a sjambok. Neighbours who heard her cries came to stop him, so were able to serve as witnesses.

After hearing the testimonies, my grandfather handed down his legendary judgement: 'The evidence is clear. You came home drunk, started a fight with your wife, and proceeded to beat her. You slapped her, and when that wasn't enough, you grabbed a sjambok and continued until neighbours heard her screams and had to stop you. Since you are clearly a very strong man and skilled at beating someone physically weaker than you, I've decided that you should fight someone bigger and stronger than you.'

He announced who the man would fight in front of everyone there – a much bigger and stronger male relative. The fight would take place in the veld, away from the eyes of children. The wife-beater did not end up fighting as much as receiving a decisive and authoritative beating. As far as we know, he never raised a hand to his wife again.

And from that day on, women who were being abused by their husbands came to my grandfather for justice.

A tale of two yards

My grandparents' home, kwaKaiser, as it was commonly called, sprawled across two regular-sized plots in Dutyini village. If you were walking from the cattle dip or the Methodist Church mission, our family home sat about a kilometre off to the left of the uneven, unmaintained gravel road that ran through the village. That gravel road stretched out like the village's spine, with houses sloping down slightly on either side. Just outside our yard was a small, shallow, makeshift dam shared by my grandparents' flock of white geese. The geese roamed the village without supervision but always made their way home in the late afternoon.

The dam was never clear, always murky and muddied, as our pigs and other animals from the community used it like a personal jacuzzi, emerging black and muddy. They would literally be as happy as pigs in mud because they were in fact pigs in mud.

The grass was short, not from mowing, but because our sheep were the lawnmowers, feeding on it each morning as they left the homestead. In winter, the grass leading to the gate turned brown, worn down by livestock hooves stomping over it twice a day.

Ours was one of the two largest residential plots in all of Dutyini. The other was right across from us, belonging to an elderly woman who lived alone. In my young eyes, she was well over a hundred years old. She'd been one of Dutyini's earliest settlers.

Her single, solitary rondavel occupying the very large plot of land looked lonely. Green aloes had been planted as a protective fence, though there was no garden to protect. Those aloes had been there for as long as I could remember, their gaps wide enough for us to slip through with our livestock, allowing them to graze in the late afternoon before taking them into our kraal. Unlike most villagers, she never scolded anyone for crossing her property with livestock, though we did so quickly and discreetly, in case she appeared.

While the garden that was never gardened was fenced off by aloes, the elderly woman's solitary rondavel had no fence, making its loneliness even more striking, with vast empty spaces surrounding the hut. Instead of glass windows, her rondavel had narrow slits on each side that were stuffed with sacks on cold days to keep the weather at bay.

Because she had lived a long life alone in the hut, there were wild rumours that she was a witch. She was old, she was dark, she was wrinkled, and she was hunched over – obvious signs she was a witch. She had outlived all her children and was all alone in the world.

My grandmother often sent me to bring her maize, milk, or food. I was always terrified to enter her house in case I was bewitched by this elderly woman. I'd run away as soon as she had taken whatever I'd brought. Her mud hut home was sparse, with only firewood, blankets, a pile of clothes, and a mattress on one side of the rondavel. There was a small table, a plastic bucket (what we called a pail), a few dishes, and a small Primus stove. Thinking back, I don't know if she actually scared me or if it was her loneliness that terrified me. I found facing her loneliness difficult to understand: How was it that an elderly person could be living alone, with no one?

Years later, I learned that she'd lost all eight of her children and had no grandchildren. People avoided her out of fear that whatever dark cloud had shadowed her life might pass to them. She'd outlived anyone of her generation, with no one to reminisce with, no one to share stories of the past. She simply shared space with the ghosts of her children, I suppose.

In contrast, our house had plenty of visitors. We had five stand-alone houses on one half of the property, while the other half had a lone rondavel. Here, we stored animal feed, saddles, grinding stones for dry mealies, and 'the planter' – a plough pulled by oxen and used to till the land in summer. It had a musky scent from the leather saddle, whips, dried cow hide, maize and everything we kept in there.

The expansive property was fenced to keep our livestock in and other people's livestock out. Another fence divided the stand-alone houses from the garden, which was sub-divided. One part, our 'orchard', had five peach trees, an orange tree that never produced, and an apple tree with the smallest green apples you'd ever seen. There was one peach tree that produced the rarest fruit in all of Dutyini – white peaches – that was protected at all costs. These peaches were very popular, not just because they were white, but were juicier and tastier than any others. My grandfather made sure that no undeserving soul ever had a taste from that tree. Still, even his authoritarian nature couldn't stop us from stealing from the forbidden tree occasionally when he was not around.

My grandmother's vegetable garden was also in the orchard. She grew pumpkins, spinach, cabbage, onions, potatoes, beetroot, and tomatoes. About 70% of the garden was reserved for planting mealies in season.

The garden also hosted the long-drop toilet, a corrugated iron structure stationed between the orchard and the maize field. When it filled up, a process that took years, a new hole would be dug nearby, and the toilet structure would be moved over it, leaving behind a quiet burial ground for generations of faeces.

At the time, I did not even know that toilet paper existed. We simply used old newspapers or any paper we could find, crumpling it between two hands furiously until it was soft enough to wipe the away remnants of whatever former nutrition we had come to deposit.

We also had two kraals – one large for cattle and a smaller one for sheep – enclosed by aloe and wooden planks. Just outside our yard were the two graves of my uncles who'd died in a horrific accident. In the village, it was believed that burying people who died violently within the homestead brought bad luck.

The yard was large and mostly bare except for patches of grass around the water tanks. The ground was hard, swept every morning after picking up fresh cow dung dropped by the cattle as they left the kraal. On days when we polished the floor of one of the huts, we'd collect the fresh, wet dung in buckets and give it to whoever had the polishing job.

On very hot days, isitshingitshane (a mini-tornado) of dust would form, swirling around then disappearing. It was believed that it was some evil spirit carrying a tokoloshe. If you saw the swirling dust early enough and threw a handful of salt into the isitshingitshane, the tokoloshe would fall out, revealing itself. I tried this a few times, but alas, no tokoloshe ever appeared. I don't know why I did it anyway because had it worked, I would have been terrified.

We had six dogs to protect the livestock and the family from potential stock thieves. Every now and then, a chicken would meet its unfortunate demise when a hawk swooped down and snatched it, sending the others clucking and scattering nervously to find hiding spots. When we spotted a hawk circling above, we'd bang on pots and yell until it flew off.

The fence and gate were almost like members of the family, serving and protecting. Every day, my grandfather inspected the fence for breaks or loose sections that might allow livestock to escape or thieves to get in. When making his rounds, I'd be with him, along with a delegation of my cousins or boys from the village who were about my age. I'd be ready to pass to him a hammer, nail, playas (pliers), pickaxe, or any tool he might need. If there was nothing to fix, he'd find something to fix.

These inspections were never silent. He'd be telling a story, making us laugh, or giving someone a tongue-lashing for being lazy. There was always someone he was roasting, and we'd laugh, happy it wasn't our turn. But you had to be strategic about laughing too much – if you seemed to enjoy it too much, he'd quickly turn his teasing on you. Laugh too little and you'd also find yourself on the receiving end.

Living at kwaKaiser was more than just growing up in a bustling homestead. It shaped who I was becoming. It was a place of unwavering constants: family, duty, and a daily rhythm that tied us together in an unspoken bond. The laughter, the endless chores, and the stories passed from one generation to the next taught me that home is a feeling.

And yet, just down the slope from all this noise and connection stood the loneliest house in Dutyini, where an elderly woman lived in silence. Her solitary rondavel, surrounded by emptiness, was a stark reminder that home can also be defined by what – or who – is missing.

Each other's entertainment

Growing up in technology-less Dutyini, the only form of entertainment we had was each other.

No one had toys or TVs. The only toys we had, we made ourselves. We raced our toy cars – made of wires, with the wheels fashioned from old fizzy-drink cans – down the first road in the village. My car was fast because I was fast, not because of any engineering trick, but because my grandfather trained me to run. When he sent me on an errand, he always made me run, saying, 'Ubuye la mathe engekomi.' ('You must return before this spit dries up.') He'd spit on the ground, and I'd run like my life depended on it.

The radio was another one of the few forms of entertainment we had. Powered by Eveready batteries, the radio wasn't always 'ever ready' and didn't last long. We would turn it on in the mornings before breakfast to catch the news. Late morning, it was time to listen to sermons and prayers. Around lunchtime, we'd listen to radio dramas on an old, simple radio. The rest of the day, the radio was switched off to preserve the batteries.

When the batteries ran low, we'd remove them from the radio and place them in direct sunlight to 'recharge', doing this over and over again until the batteries were too drained. Then we'd go a few days without radio until we could buy new batteries.

The radio signal would be much stronger those first few days of a new one, and the older it got, the sound deteriorated and so did the signal. We'd also have to fiddle with the aerial much more frequently.

In the evenings, the radio came back on for *Apha Naphaya* ('Here and There') – current affairs on Radio Transkei, followed by choir music and the popular *Imiphanga* – the death notices! People gathered around the radio in the kitchen, eating and listening. There were never less than ten people eating in the kitchen, and the sound of spoons was in slight competition with the radio as the plates emptied, each spoon striking the bottom of an enamel plate.

Occasionally, I would hear my grandparents gasping when they heard that someone they knew had passed. They would start making arrangements to visit the bereaved family. There were no newspapers in Dutyini, and even if there were, few people could read them. If an old newspaper did find its way to us, it was used to roll BB Best Blend tobacco or as toilet paper in the long-drop.

This was family time, a chance for us all to be together. My grandparents sat and ate at the small kitchen table with two grown-up guests. My sister and I, and the younger relatives who always ended up at our home, sat on the floor to eat, while the teenagers and slightly older family members sat on benches against the wall. It was here, eating and listening, that family stories often spilled out, blending with the news and dramas of the day, shaping us as much as the crackling radio did.

We'd hear stories from our older cousins – what had happened on their way to or from the river. At some stage, someone would tell us a fable involving a jackal and fox, with some lesson about life.

Then it would be time for prayers. Hymns would begin, and if someone was off-key, my grandfather would stop the singing and get everyone to start over again until the melody was right.

In the end, all we had were each other, with stories passed from one generation to the next. And it was my mother who knew this best.

Mother, the storyteller

Stories remind us never to forget where we come from, nor the long road we've had to travel to get to where we are. You may have walked slower than others, may have faced obstacles they couldn't imagine, but you got there. That's what stories do for us.

Amid the everyday storytelling that filled our lives growing up in Dutyini were my mother's stories. Her stories were different to the rest, at least for me. She wasn't just telling tales; she was shaping memories, teaching us where we came from and how to find strength in our roots. She had an active imagination and would make up her own unique stories or retell tales she'd got from different sources within the community.

Even when I was much older, whenever we asked my mother to tell a story, she'd first put on an air of reluctance, as if she was being bothered, as if storytelling was the last thing she wanted to do. Her face would fall as she'd say, 'Hayi, suka,' with a finality that seemed to close the matter. But if you knew her, you'd see the hidden smile, as if the idea was already warming her up.

Though soft-spoken, her 'no' was always clear. Even when she raised her voice, it sounded strained, as if her vocal cords were naturally restricted to a certain sound barrier. We knew when we were in trouble or when she was shouting at us, but it had nothing to do with the loudness of her voice.

If you were smart, you'd know not to push too hard. You simply had to nudge her enough, like pushing a boulder that's nearly at the top of a hill – one last gentle push and gravity would do the rest, sending it rolling with unstoppable force. Once her storytelling began, it tumbled along with excitement.

When she started a story, she'd often be sitting on the couch, her hands resting on her belly, her head leaning back, her long, thick dreadlocks cascading around her shoulders. She'd begin slowly, even reluctantly, and you'd feel the temptation to hurry her along, but that was unnecessary. Soon, she'd lean forward, her hands coming to life, shaping the story alongside her voice. The cadence of her voice would ebb and flow, and sometimes, she'd even stand up to act out parts of the tale. Laughter would always follow.

As I got older, when I visited my mother, she'd stop me from leaving to see my friends by starting a story. It was her way of trapping me and drawing us into togetherness.

Storytelling is often described as a natural Xhosa trait. While not exclusive to the amaXhosa, there's a unique charisma and even unintended humour in the way we tell even the most tragic stories. My favourite TikTok storytellers are those who tell their tales in isiXhosa. It's not uncommon to see comments from people saying, 'I have no idea what you said but I couldn't help but be captivated by the story.'

Once, when my mother found out I was shortlisted for the Sunday Times Non-Fiction Prize, she told me that I loved telling stories when I was a child. Before she was forced to leave my sister Siki and me with her parents to work in Mdantsane, we'd lived together, and I was already obsessed with stories.

Not only did I love to tell stories, but every night before bed, I'd beg her for a story. She would tell it and pretend to be falling asleep halfway through, and I'd cry, shaking her awake to finish. I'd even threaten to go to my aunt, Nolulama, for bedtime stories if she continued to fall asleep. She'd laugh, 'wake up' and continue. I would stay awake the whole time and when she was done, I would ask her questions about the story until I was satisfied.

It did not end there. The next morning, it was my turn, and I would recount the same story back to her. Sometimes I would ask her to repeat a story she'd told before, and if she skipped any detail (something she often did to tease me), I'd make her go back and retell it properly.

We really do live in stories. The stories we create about people make them feel more real to us than the flesh and blood they're made of. When they're no longer physically present, stories are all we have left of them.

My mother's storytelling didn't just entertain me as a child – it taught me the power of words and memory. And though I don't think I inherited her talent for oral storytelling – her ability to tell a story so well that it enthrals her audience – I do think that she is why I write.

In fact, she wasn't just the person who encouraged me to start reading – she outright forced me to. And while I resented it at the time, I will forever be grateful for that gift. What started as something I hated became an obsession. Through books, I discovered stories about worlds and possibilities I never imagined existed. Her stories, I realise now, were her way of showing me that the world was far bigger than the small one I could see in Dutyini and Mdantsane.

My mother and the lost horse, Bhayibhile

Parents have a way of one-upping you, even unintentionally. That's why parents will tell stories about how they walked to school 20 kilometres in the snow while fighting off polar bears, even if they lived in a desert. Or they'll say: 'Anything you can do, I can do better,' or, 'The worst thing that's happened to you? My experience was worse.' My mother is no different.

In my book *These Things Really Do Happen To Me*, there is a story about the time I had to chase my grandfather's horse across the veld for three hours. I was ten years old. After reading this chapter, my mother laughed and told me she had a story that was better than mine.

Hold your horses, so to speak. First, some background.

Alfred Kaiser Boyce, my grandfather, loved his horses. When I was a child, his favourite was Commando but back then, when his daughter was young, his favourite was Bhayibhile. This horse held a special place in his heart, and no one but my grandfather was allowed to ride him. There was nothing more important to Tat'omkhulu than that horse.

Known for his elegance, Bhayibhile had a graceful gait that

people admired as he trotted through the village. He was tall, tame, and beloved by everyone who saw him. Bhayibhile was so well-trained, he could have belonged to the Queen of England.

One night, when Tat'omkhulu was returning from town, Bhayibhile tripped on a rock and both horse and rider fell into the river. Tat'omkhulu hit his head on a rock and lost consciousness, and by the time he came to his senses, he was bleeding and disoriented. He picked himself up, ears ringing. The water on his face felt warm, which was strange because the river was cold. When he touched his face, he realised that it was his own thick blood.

Not only was he dizzy, but it was dark, and he hadn't brought a torch with him. He dreaded having to try walk home. There were no houses for a couple of kilometres after the river and the footpath to the village was on an uphill walk on a rough terrain.

But when he mustered the strength to stand, he noticed Bhayibhile standing on the opposite bank, waiting for him. I don't know if horses pray, but it felt like it to Tat'omkhulu.

Most horses, when they lose their rider, go home alone, alerting people to search for the fallen rider. But Bhayibhile stayed. My grandfather knew he wouldn't have made it home on foot in the condition he was in. From that day, his love for Bhayibhile was far greater than he thought possible.

Now that you understand how special this horse was, I'll share the story my mother claimed is better than mine.

In the summer months, my grandfather's cattle and horses would be sent up the steep Ntsizwa mountain to stay with relatives who had better grazing land. It was a six-hour trek up the mountain and a six-hour journey back down. Ntsizwa was significantly more fertile than Dutyini and its rivers flowed with cold, sweet waters that could be enjoyed during the trip.

One evening, some boys from the family that was keeping Tat'omkhulu's livestock arrived with bad news: Bhayibhile had gone missing. After two days of searching, the boys hadn't found them and suspected the horses might have tried to make their way home to Dutyini. But the horses were not there.

My grandfather was anxious about Bhayibhile and he commissioned my mother, Nonceba, then thirteen, and her sixteen-year-old cousin, Mandlakayise, to search for him. They were to leave with the boys before first light, as the first cocks crowed, to head back to Ntsizwa and look around the neighbouring villages for the horse.

Ntsizwa had a diverse mix of people who lived together across different villages. Those who had settled there were amaXesibe, amaHlubi, amaBhaca and abeSuthu – but everyone spoke isiXesibe, which is more closely related to isiMpondo than it is to isiXhosa.

To hike Ntsizwa, you had to carry two strong sticks, usually a fighting stick and a knobkerrie. These were needed to help you navigate the steep paths, and for self-defence. Sometimes you encountered boys from another village who wanted to start mischief, and you had to stand your ground. The heavy-duty knobkerrie was also used for hunting small animals on the way. I was familiar with this route my mother was telling me about, having trekked it myself with my cousins decades later.

After summiting the mountain, my mother and bhut' Mandlakayise had a long walk before encountering the first village, eMapeleni. This was where their relatives, Mr Sgwebela and his family, lived and looked after Tat'omkhulu's livestock.

For days, bhuti, my mother and two of Sgwebela's sons went from village to village, searching for the horses. They crossed the length and breadth of each village and searched the surrounding fields. At dusk each day, they'd return to the home of the family keeping the livestock. After three days, a visitor at Sgwebela home suggested that they try Lisuthu village because, the man said, 'The Sotho in these parts are well known for livestock theft, especially horses.'

The next day, they searched the expansive Lisuthu veld before entering the village. They came upon a homestead with a large stable of horses. The home was bustling with celebration, with many people drinking. They found the man of the house and asked if Bhayibhile had perhaps wandered into their property and ended up among their many horses, but he was emphatic that every horse in the yard belonged to him.

As they turned to leave, something caught my mother's eye. A horse that looked strikingly similar to Bhayibhile was among the other horses. But instead of being grey, this horse was dark. What stood out even more was that this horse was wearing horseshoes. My grandfather's horses always wore horseshoes, but up in Ntsizwa, it was unheard of for people to shoe their horses. The sight struck my mother as odd: a horse that resembled Bhayibhile, just the wrong colour, and the only one in the yard with horseshoes? Her suspicions began to grow.

As they walked out of the gate, they decided to test their suspicions and called out, 'Bhayibhile!' They made the familiar sounds used to summon my grandfather's horses: 'Qhoo! Qhoo! Drii! Driii!' Almost instantly, the horse with the horseshoes pricked its ears, raised its head, and neighed loudly. It even began to paw at the ground with its front hoof!

They were even more suspicious now. But they were just children and couldn't confront the owner during the celebration, so they returned to their host family for the fourth night. When they arrived, they were surprised to find that Tat'omkhulu was there. Before he could even ask, they told him about the horse they had seen at Lisuthu village.

Wasting no time, my grandfather announced they would head back to check. The village was a long distance away. Tat'omkhulu and Mr Sgwebela rode their own horses, while my mother and bhut' Mandlakayise shared one.

When they finally arrived at the homestead, the celebrations were still going, with drinking and traditional dancing taking place.

Tat'omkhulu called out to one of the men he'd heard was a well-known livestock thief, as well as several others.

He exchanged no pleasantries. 'I've heard that you're a thief. You will find my horse and give it back to me or I will have every single one of you arrested.'

'I promise you tat'uSnama, there is no horse that is yours here. All these horses belong to this house,' the man replied.

Tat'omkhulu persisted. 'What do you then suggest I do to you if I find my horse amongst these horses?'

'You should have us arrested, but I promise you that your horse isn't here,' the man insisted.

With that, Tat'omkhulu led them to the horses.

He had a specific praise for each one of his horses, and Bhayibhile was no exception. Once he got to the horses, he began to shout his praises and ululations: 'Bhayibhile! Wena, Bhayibhile yamakholwa!' ('Bible! You believer's Bible!') He used the sounds the horse would recognise: 'Qhoo! Qhoo! Drii! Driii!' then shouted, 'Suka sebethu uthath' bheshu lakho sigoduke kukude, Mzintlava hayibo!' ('Take your loin cloth and let's go. Mzintlava River is far, hayibo!')

Bhayibhile lifted his head, wiggled his ears, flared his nostrils, neighed, and dug the ground with his hoof. He ran over to Tat'omkhulu immediately and brushed himself against him.

'What do you have to say now?' said Tat'omkhulu, stroking his horse's face.

The man mumbled excuses, claiming he didn't know how the horse got there and that it must have wandered over.

Tat'omkhulu demanded, 'Why is the colour different if you don't know how it got here? Why is it dyed? Did it dye itself with its hands?'

They had no answer.

'Here's what's going to happen,' my grandfather said. 'First, you're going to feed my horse and the others we brought with us. Second, you're going to slaughter a sheep and give me the whole carcass. Third, you're going to give me money to replace Bhayibhile's horseshoes.'

They did as he requested. Tat'omkhulu's reputation as someone not to be messed with was well-established in the region, and after that, it only grew.

After my mother told me this story, I conceded that her story was, in fact, much better than mine.

This story, like so many of my mother's, was not just about a horse. It was about character, respect, and the quiet power of not backing down. And maybe that's why it stayed with me. It reminded me that true authority comes not from fear, but from a steadfast sense of self and an unshakeable ability to stand firm and command respect.

The aftermath

When they arrived at Sgwebela's homestead that evening with Bhayibhile trailing behind, everyone felt the tension radiating from Tat'omkhulu. He was not relieved to have recovered his horse; instead, he was furious at the audacity of those who'd stolen, and worse, taken his favourite horse. Even the sheep slaughtered for him and the money for the horseshoes did little to simmer his anger.

At the homestead, tat'uSgwebela removed the saddle from Tat'omkhulu's horse and began brushing it down, while my grandfather walked around, looking at the livestock on the property and inspecting each of his animals carefully. He paid particular attention to the cows with young calves. The summer grazing grounds in Ntsizwa were fertile, and there was no reason the livestock shouldn't be well-fattened after grazing on those grasslands.

He was not happy with what he saw.

Summoning tat'uSgwebela and his sons, my grandfather began an inquisition.

The calves were thin, while the oxen, bulls, and cows without calves looked properly fattened. Tat'omkhulu concluded that

Sgwebela was taking advantage and over-milking the cows, leaving little for the calves to feed on.

'What did I say to you when I asked you to look after my cattle?' Tat'omkhulu asked.

Sgwebela replied, 'Sorry, Snama, sorry, Radu. You said the livestock should be kept in the kraal at night and not left to roam, especially near Lisuthu village. And you told us to leave enough milk for the calves and not to over-milk the cows.'

'Then what is so difficult about following the rules you know and agreed to?'

Sgwebela tried to explain, 'No, Snama, these boys are young …'

Tat'omkhulu interrupted him: 'Clearly, you fear your sons. Since you are scared of them, I'll handle it.' He sat Sgwebela and his sons down on a bench outside the kraal and launched into a vicious verbal onslaught.

'First all you, you drink ijiki (traditional beer) with these sons of yours, and you're busy smoking intsangu (weed) with them. What grown man smokes intsangu with his sons? How do you expect them to respect you? Clearly you don't want to be a man; you want to be a boy, like them. I make you a respectable man in this village with livestock. I let you ride my horses, and you get to ride different ones whenever you like – you enjoy the honours of a rich man. And this is how you thank me? I had to get my young daughter to walk all the way up the mountain to come look for a horse you weren't even trying to find. What is wrong with you? A little girl did what you, a grown man, failed to do.'

Father and sons shifted uncomfortably, staring at the ground.

'I give you sheep at the end of the year to thank you for looking after my livestock. This is how you thank me? This ends today.'

They understood immediately. Today, Christmas was over. Tat'omkhulu didn't have to make explicit threats; everyone knew he could take his livestock from Sgwebela's care and give it to another family in the village. This would leave Sgwebela without cattle for ploughing his fields, without cows to milk, and without milk to sell for income. He'd have no horses to ride and would be thrust back into poverty in an instant.

Tat'omkhulu did not have to resort to this threat, but it hung in the air like a sword about to behead a man.

Even despite his dissatisfaction with tat'uSgwebela, when Tat'omkhulu, my mother, and bhut' Mandlakayise prepared to leave the next day, he left the family with a leg of the sheep he had demanded from the thieves. He had made his point and exacted his justice, but he wasn't there to leave anyone starving.

As they mounted their horses – my grandfather on Bhayibhile and my mother and Mandlakayise on another – Tat'omkhulu delivered his final parting words: 'If I ever come back here and there's a missing cow, a dead horse, or if my calves are thin, you will see who I am.'

From that day on, according to my mother, tat'uSgwebela became the model caretaker of Tat'omkhulu's livestock. His vigilance was unmatched, and the reputation of my grandfather as a man not to be crossed remained firmly intact.

Decades later, when I was old enough to take trips up to Ntsizwa to drop off or collect my grandfather's livestock, I was treated like royalty. Royalty that slept on the floor, wrapped in flea-infested blankets – but royalty, nonetheless. The respect and reverence my grandfather had earned extended to me, his grandchild, simply because I carried his name and legacy.

Tat'omkhulu's actions weren't just about the stolen horse.

They were about setting a standard. Through him, I learned that respect is earned through courage, fairness, and the resolute defence of what is rightfully yours.

The terrifying English words

Much of my childhood in Dutyini involved running errands for my grandparents. In fact, Alfred Kaiser Boyce was notorious for sending his grandkids on errands all over the village on a daily basis. As a disciplinarian, he was stern yet loving, and had very strict beliefs about what boys should do. But while my grandfather's tasks tested my stamina and obedience, the errands given to me by my grandmother, Vuyelwa Victoria Boyce, were often more nerve-wracking because they tested my English – which barely existed. All I could say in English was, 'What is your name?', 'My name is Khayalethu' and of course, 'Yes' and 'No'. That was it.

Makhulu's errands often involved more English words, as they usually meant trips to the local general store owned by the Chanca family, which was filled with items labelled in English. The English language can be a great enemy to a child who does not speak it or even understand it. It is especially difficult when you are sent to buy something with an unfamiliar name.

Each morning, after waking up in the rondavel where I slept when cousins visited (which was often and always), or in my uncle Nyameko Boyce's stand-alone four-corner structure, I knew I needed to be ready for a jog to a relative's house, to deliver or collect a parcel or to relay a message. There were no telephones of any kind in the entire village, so it was only natural that I became the living, breathing communication system and unofficial courier service provider.

My greatest fear was forgetting what I had been sent to buy by the time I reached the shops, especially if I got distracted and chatted to friends on the way. The worst items to be sent to buy were those with big English names that you couldn't even pronounce or remember. In my case, *bicarbonate of soda*.

Makhulu would double-check before I left: 'What did I say you must go buy?'

'Bicarbonate of soda,' I'd repeat.

And as I ran out of the house and across the grassless yard, I'd chant to myself, 'Bicarbonate of soda, bicarbonate of soda, bicarbonate of soda, bicarbonate of soda,' making a song out of it so I wouldn't forget. By the time I got to the shop, I would have repeated 'bicarbonate of soda' some 500 times – if no one distracted me on the way.

The biggest problem was overconfidence. If I thought that I'd repeated this unfamiliar name enough times for it to be etched into my memory and allowed myself to be distracted – whether chatting to a friend, or joining a quick soccer game on the dirt road – I risked forgetting the name entirely. Realising I'd forgotten it was terrifying but I'd still continue to the shops, hoping I'd remember once I got there.

Forgetting meant a guaranteed scolding and another trip back to the shops. But going back home empty-handed and confessing you forgot was always the better option – it was a worse crime to guess and buy the wrong item. On a few occasions, I confused tartaric acid with bicarbonate of soda and when I got home, Makhulu would be upset and I'd have to run back again to the shop to exchange it for bicarbonate of soda.

The only thing worse than buying the wrong thing because you didn't know the English terms was being sent to buy paraffin. There was nothing fundamentally wrong or difficult about buying paraffin. And at least you'd never forget what you were there to buy because when you got to the shops, you were holding an old 2-litre plastic milk bottle without a lid – a repurposed paraffin container. But the smell of paraffin clung to your hands as you'd switched the container from one hand to the other while heading to the store.

Once you got to the shop, you would tell them how much paraffin you wanted and they would pump it from a big enamel container into your mbombozi (a repurposed plastic milk container). Walking home, you would carry it with utmost care because, of course, none of these mbombozis ever seemed to have their lids on anymore. You had to make sure it didn't slip from your fingers, because it was heavy and you were small. You had to be extra cautious when switching it from one hand to the other. One wrong move, and you'd lose half your load – and scolding was guaranteed when you got back if you did.

While carrying this precious commodity for the Primus stove or paraffin lamp, you could not allow yourself to be easily startled. Dogs barking as you passed by had to be ignored, and any temptation to get into any fights with boys your age had to be ignored too. A fight could mean the tragedy of spilled paraffin. Now you'd get in trouble for getting into a fight and spilling paraffin. Even if you won the fight, the loss of the paraffin would outweigh a thousand victories.

The greatest horror was spilling the whole bottle of paraffin on your way home if you fell. At this point, you might as well be proactive and head to the garden to find a stick for your own beating. Returning home empty-handed meant dragging your feet, leaning against walls as you dragged your body into the house to report the great crime of paraffin spillage.

But often you did not even need to confess. Where the paraffin spilled on you, the spot on your leg would be extra shiny. Before you'd have a chance to say anything, the look on your face, the scratching of the wall with your back and your guilty, too-close proximity to the door would have been its own confession already. When you stood too close to the door, it was a telltale sign that you wanted to bolt out of the door before a slipper came flying at you after you'd reported what had happened.

'Where is the paraffin?' you'd be asked.

Even though you had already worked out what to say once you got home, you would still give a hesitant answer. You would make up some elaborate story about a dog or boys who were chasing you, and how you'd fallen and the paraffin had spilled as a result – all this while creeping slowly towards the open door.

It would be a relief to be sent back to the shop without a beating – but you'd still be concerned that it would happen when you returned. This time, you'd take every precaution, even securing the mbombozi in a plastic bag. Luckily, I have never heard of anyone spilling paraffin twice in one day. That would be the horror of horrors.

Looking back, those trips to fetch paraffin were lessons in focus and responsibility. The road was full of distractions like barking dogs, playful boys, the temptation to stop and rest – but the task at hand always mattered more. You have to protect what you're entrusted with.

Say my name

I've been told by about a dozen people that I rarely use their names – unless I need their attention. So, when I do say the name of someone I interact with often, not just as a function, but in the middle of a conversation, they notice. This was something I was unaware of doing until it was pointed out to me. Apparently, it's a strange and unusual habit.

I recall having a conversation with a friend, Celeste Khumalo.

'Look at you, Celeste. That's really good,' I said.

Her response took me by surprise. 'Oh my God, you said my name. You never say my name. I like how you say it. I mean, you do say it, but only when you're calling me – like at a restaurant when you want me to pass the salt or if I'm across the room. But never in the middle of a conversation.'

'Really?' I asked. She wasn't the first person to point this out, but hearing it again made me reflect that there might be something unusual about this.

I have realised that people place a lot of value on hearing their names spoken – not as a summons, reprimand, or demand, but simply for their sake. Perhaps it makes them feel seen.

But why don't I do it more often? Why do I hesitate to say

someone's name unless it's necessary? I think it has something to do with where I grew up and how names were used.

In Dutyini, I didn't know the names of at least 90% of the grown-ups in the village. What I did know were their children's or grandchildren's names. Somehow, I knew my grandparents' names, but that's because my grandfather's name was always on everyone's lips.

His initials – AKB for Alfred Kaiser Boyce – were branded on every one of his livestock: cattle, sheep, and horses. I often watched as the animals were branded with his name. I always knew that his name was Kaiser because people would ask me, 'Are you Kaiser's grandson?' It was impossible not to know his name.

But for most elders in the village, their names were a mystery. Gogo Ma'am was one of my grandfather's sisters and as a child, I had no reason to think that her name was not Gogo Ma'am because everyone called her that. I didn't know that her actual name was Nomkhizo until I was almost 20.

This wasn't unusual in Dutyini. Old people were never referred to by their names. To an outsider, it might seem strange, but where I am from, it was normal.

If a teenager was sent to deliver a message to my grandfather, their parents would say, 'Yiya kutata kaNyameko' ('Go to Nyameko's father') – Nyameko being my grandfather's last-born son.

Uncle Nyameko lived with us, so his name was used as a reference. His oldest son, by contrast, lived far away in Mdantsane with his older sister, my aunt, Nolulama.

However, for younger children, the instructions would be different: 'Yiya kutat'omkhulu kaKhayalethu.' ('Go to Khayalethu's grandfather.')

Life is like that sometimes

All the children in the village knew each other, so our names were the most practical identifiers. Knowing the names of elders simply wasn't necessary.

One of my grandfather's sisters lived to the age of 96. I was in my late twenties when she passed. I only found out at her funeral that her name was Nofour – the fourth-born child. We had simply called her Khulu or Makhulu waseSibongiseni ('the grandmother from Sibongiseni') after the homestead where she lived. Sibongiseni was the only shop in the area, serving the nearby villages of Nodongwe and Majalumani.

I suspect names were considered sacred – something that couldn't just be uttered by anyone. Perhaps the right to say someone's name had to be earned. It may also have been a sign of knowing someone long enough or intimately enough to address them by name.

Even though my grandfather was commonly known as 'K' (for Kaiser), only the elderly referred to him in that way, and never to his face. Most people addressed him by his clan name, Snama or as Bawo Boyce (Mr Boyce).

In fact, his own sisters never called him by name. They always to referred to him uyise kaNomakhosi (Nomakhosi's father), after the name of his first-born child who had passed on before I was born.

So it's no wonder my grandfather's sister became known as Gogo Ma'am. She was a lively, kind, and talkative woman who adored me immensely. Like all her siblings, she had light-brown eyes and a fair complexion. Even when she removed her false teeth, her charm remained intact. She was a granny and a teacher – not just any teacher, but a principal.

In Dutyini, saying someone's name meant you truly knew them, beyond the surface, beyond their role.

Perhaps that's why I use names sparingly. I still hold them as something sacred, a gift to give. Maybe one day I will grow out of Dutyini and start using people's names more.

Gogo Ma'am's school

My mother had made sure I started school at least two years earlier than most, giving me a head start. Perhaps she wanted me to socialise early or find a way to contain my restless energy. In Dutyini, there were no preschools – you simply began school when the time came.

As the youngest in my class, I suppose I was bound to think of myself as somehow special. Even at that young age, I had a sense of exceptionalism. My quarrels were often with older boys, and it wasn't long before I learned to stand up for myself. I thought it was because I was a damn good fighter, but looking back, it was more likely that they feared my grandfather. If I'd dug deeper, I would have realised it wasn't exceptionalism at all – it was the privilege of being my grandfather's grandchild, with all the reverence and protection that came with proximity to a man like him.

While living with my grandparents as a snotty-nosed seven-year-old boy, my mother decided it might be better for me to complete my Standard 1 education in Ndzongiseni – a village on the foothills of the Ntsizwa mountain in what is now known as the Eastern Cape, a province chiefly populated by the Xhosa.

This part of the world was Transkei – a 'country within a country', so to speak. The government laughably required you to have a passport to leave Transkei, a passport only recognised within the confines of apartheid South Africa.

Transkei is home to many tribal identities, such as amaMpondo, abaThembu, amaHlubi, amaBhaca, amaMpondomise, and amaXesibe, as well as others who spoke variations of isiXhosa. My family's identity was no less complex: on my father's side, we claimed abaThembu roots through the Madiba clan name, while my mother's side hailed from EmaXesibeni through the Snama clan.

Many knew that giving their child a shot at an education offered a path to some form of success, so they did everything possible to provide it. This was how I came to attend a school run by my great-aunt. Known as isikolo sika Gogo Ma'am (Gogo Ma'am's school), it was not really hers; the school actually belonged to the government of Transkei, but she led it with authority and care.

In some ways, Ndzongiseni felt forgotten by the rest of the world. Every hardship seemed to conspire with the next to make things harder for those of us living far from the main roads and resources. The school was, like much of Ndzongiseni, at the mercy of the elements. Although land had been allocated to it, there wasn't enough indoor space, so not all grades were housed in any kind of building. It was not unusual to have classes under the stereotypical African tree, with the teacher pointing at a blackboard mounted on an easel. This was my first introduction to school at Ndzongiseni.

The sudden afternoon summer thunderstorms would often force us to vacate our 'classrooms' from beneath some tree. We would pile into a neighbouring hut or a classroom already filled with another grade. On particularly cold and rainy days, some of the families living next to the school would be asked if they could host a class in one of their huts.

I remember one rainy afternoon where chickens ran into the classroom with us – thirty-odd kids, a teacher, and a flock of chickens all together in the same space. Unlike children from the city, who might have been horrified, we were unperturbed by the sight of chickens invading our space. We coexisted with them, at least until one of them became a succulent meal. I felt like they lived a nervous existence, knowing one of their own might disappear from the flock, never to be seen again.

That ability to adapt and make do was something I only fully appreciated later in life. Gogo Ma'am's school may not have had the comforts or facilities of a city school, but it was there that I first understood the resilience and creativity of our community.

For many years, I believed my place in the world was earned through my own strength and intelligence. But my time at Gogo Ma'am's school taught me that privilege comes in many forms. Sometimes, privilege is the shelter of a name – like my grandfather's in Dutyini, a protection I lacked when I arrived in Ndzongiseni. I wasn't as exceptional as I thought. I simply had a grandfather whose name carried weight.

Yet even in Ndzongiseni, I was fortunate. The school principal was my grandfather's sister. It was a reminder that while strength and hard work matter, so too does the legacy we inherit and the shoulders we stand on.

To Gogo Ma'am's house

Every Sunday afternoon, as the shadows of the Ntsizwa mountain crept across the Dutyini maize-planting fields, I'd pack my bag for the week and start making my way to Gogo Ma'am's house. Her home, on the slope of the hill, was a couple of kilometres from my grandparents' homestead.

Often, though, I would walk up to Gogo Ma'am's house with an older cousin the day before. Sometimes, my grandfather would take me on horseback, an excuse for him to see his sister. He'd hoist me onto the front, letting me hold the reins and making me feel as though I was guiding Commando, his favourite horse at the time.

Our journey together became a ritual of sorts, with my grandfather telling stories or jokes. As we rode along, I noticed how everyone greeted him. 'Molo, molo, molo, Snama!' they'd call, or 'Molo, molo, molo, Boyce!' It seemed everyone wanted a moment of his time, and he gave it generously. He was both feared and loved in the community, and that aura of respect wrapped itself around me too. The confidence I carried as a child was largely due to his influence and the way others treated him, and indirectly, me.

It wasn't just clothes I packed every Sunday, but also food supplies from home – fresh veggies, mealie meal, a live chicken, sugar, tomatoes, and so on. The general dealer in Ndzongiseni didn't always have what we needed, so we brought our own supplies.

I wasn't the only child travelling to Gogo Ma'am's house on Sundays. My cousins, Nosipho, Ndiviwe and Nosisa Dandala, also attended the primary school she led. I was the baby in the group, so most of the heavy tasks went to them.

During the week, the five of us would sleep in a single rented rondavel in Ndzongiseni. Gogo Ma'am would take the bed, and the rest of us would sleep on mattresses spread across the floor. That rondavel was sparsely furnished and served as bedroom, kitchen, lounge, and bathroom for all of us. When we woke up reluctantly in the morning, we'd wash in a shallow plastic tub called the waskom (washbasin), heating water on the paraffin stove in a large pot, then each taking turns. Washing was a whole process. You'd kneel beside the tub, scooping water with a face cloth to wash your face and upper body. Then, the finale – standing in the shallow water to wash your legs and feet, bending over and balancing in the small tub.

There's a story I've been told about how I would impersonate Gogo Ma'am washing her under parts. She would stand, feet planted firmly in the waskom, with a large towel wrapped around her, legs bent. I'd mimic her, and the adults would laugh and then tell me to stop. Of course, how was I not to see her washing if we were all in one room?

Gogo Ma'am had lost her husband long before I was born, as well as her beautiful daughter, sis' Thembisa, to a tragic accident. Thembisa had been confined to a wheelchair after a tree fell on her. I remembered her as the most glamorous and beautiful young woman I had ever seen. She had a glorious smile, a big perm, and wore big earrings. She sadly passed away a few years later.

Even with these losses, Gogo Ma'am carried herself with strength and took charge of everything, especially the school.

The uncooperative potatoes

About 300 steep metres from Gogo Ma'am's house was the bus stop, where we'd catch a ride to another village for school on Mondays. The journey began early – by 4 am, the household was already awake. Each of us would take turns washing in the waskom before we set off, with Gogo Ma'am leading the way.

We'd walk up the steep gravel road to the makeshift bus stop, each of us carrying our bag of clothes and a Checkers bag of groceries for the week.

The steep rocky road had little dongas formed by rivulets after it rained. We hated walking uphill to the bus stop so early in the morning, long before the sunrise. The winters were particularly unkind because we would have to walk on frosty grass in the early-morning winter darkness.

I was seven years old, and, as the youngest, I often carried the least. On this particular Monday, I had been given the task of looking after potatoes wrapped in a tied-up plastic shopping bag. No one called these bags 'plastics'. Rather, they were called 'Checkers', simply because Checkers was a big grocery-store chain and one of the first retailers to brand their plastic bags. No matter what plastic bag you had, even if it was from another store, it was called a Checkers.

The bus stop itself wasn't a designated spot – it was simply a convenient gathering place where villagers waited for the first bus from Dutyini to Mount Ayliff. From there, we'd switch to another bus bound for Ndzongiseni, ready to begin the week.

We waited at the makeshift station until the first bus arrived to take us to Mount Ayliff. This was the first leg of our journey, and thankfully, the bus wasn't unbearably full that day.

When we arrived at the bus station in Mount Ayliff, we got off and prepared to catch another bus that would take us to our final destination, Ndzongiseni. The station buzzed with fruit sellers and passengers, as it always did on a Monday morning.

The second bus, the one to Ndzongiseni, was much fuller. To make space for others, Gogo Ma'am let me sit on her lap. As the bus navigated its way out of Mount Ayliff, we passed familiar landmarks. On the left side of the road was the KwaMenyo Mobil petrol station. On the right, the untouched natural vegetation stretched out, a reminder of the beauty and vastness of our part of the world. The bus descended steadily along the slope.

Then, suddenly, everything went wrong.

As we reached the slight bend in the road, two things happened at once: the wheels locked up, and the brakes failed entirely. As the driver lost control and the bus sped downhill and off the road into shrubbery, the beautiful scenery I was admiring stopped being beautiful. I heard women screaming and praying. 'Sizobhubha nkosi yam!' ('My God, we are going to die!') someone cried.

I remember seeing the driver on his feet, pumping his foot against the unresponsive brake. He was wearing a trench coat, and his hands gripped the wheel as he tried to wrestle the bus

Life is like that sometimes

back under control. The bus bounced over rocks and shrubs, and we were thrown from side to side. With each jolt, the passengers' cries grew louder, filled with cries of 'Thixo!' and 'Nkosi enofefe!' ('God!' and 'God of Mercies!').

Just before we plunged into what looked like a massive donga, the driver managed to steer the bus towards a boulder. The impact was abrupt, slamming us to a stop. We were all saved.

Without hesitation, everyone then got off the bus in a manner I would not describe as orderly. I suppose, the last place anyone wanted to be was on the bus.

Except for me.

I stayed on the bus for one simple reason: the potatoes. As soon as we had started our descent to what seemed like certain doom, my bag of potatoes had slipped from my grasp and scattered all over the floor of the bus. Now I had a mission: leave no potato behind. I had one job and I was not going to fail at it.

So while everyone else was rejoicing and thanking God outside, I was down on my hands and knees, picking up each precious potato, oblivious to everything else.

At some point, Gogo Ma'am realised that I was unaccounted for and she panicked, thinking that I was injured or dead on the bus. When she found me, I was still busy gathering potatoes.

'Get off the bus!' she shouted, furious.

'But Gogo Ma'am, the potatoes!' I insisted.

She was even angrier then, telling me to leave those bloody potatoes and dragging me off the bus.

Years later, my mother would still recall this story as Gogo Ma'am had told it to her. Always shaking her head and laughing, she'd start the story with: 'This child! What potatoes were these that were so important?'

Legends of witches

If Dutyini was a long way off the N2, Ndzongiseni was even further. Reaching it meant crossing rivers and climbing hills, the thatched-roofed rondavel homesteads dotting the foothills of the expansive Ntsizwa mountain. On the opposite side of Ntsizwa lay a dense forest, where myths and fears lived as thick as the trees.

We heard rumours, as children, that if you went deep enough into the forest you would be captured by powerful witches who would turn you into isithunzela (a zombie). The wild, untamed parts of the forest were to be avoided at all costs. These legends were etched in my mind from as early as I can remember, just as they were for every other child in the village. Only the most powerful witches, we were told, gathered there to perform spells, and if you wandered in by accident, you'd never be seen again. Even the strongest amagqirha (traditional healers) were said to be powerless against the spells cast by these scary witches.

Their powers were beyond comprehension. They could send lightning to strike your house in broad daylight, even when no clouds were in sight. Although no one I knew had ever witnessed it, everyone believed it could happen. People said it had occurred once, far away in a village called Nodwengu, where lightning struck without warning. Everyone knew someone who knew someone who had seen it happen, so we believed it.

Unlike the witches in Western stories who flew on broomsticks, ours supposedly flew inside (preferably brown) loaves of bread. They could fit inside these loaves by casting a spell that made them small enough to fit inside. While Jesus could feed a horde of five thousand people with just five loaves of bread, he was no match for the witches who could achieve something even more miraculous: Bread Airways.

Bread Airways could only fly in the early hours between 1 am and 3 am. If anyone happened to be outside and look up and see them with their human eyes, the spell would break. The loaf of bread would come crashing down, with the witches falling out and returning to normal size before hitting the ground.

Having their bread seen while it was in mid-flight was apparently the witches' worst nightmare. They were said to cast spells around the bread to shield it from the view of mortals. But occasionally, an incompetent witch would forget to cast the invisibility spell. Again, no one I knew had ever given an eyewitness account of witches falling off loaves of brown bread, but someone always claimed to know someone who had seen it.

The witches needed Bread Airways to fly from village to village, picking up others to go to their witch meetings in the forest, where they turned various people into zombies who could never escape. Some witches even rode baboons. Apparently.

Life in Ndzongiseni

Beyond the legends of witches in the area, it felt as if time itself stood still in Ndzongiseni. In villages like this, far from the national road, progress happened slowly, if at all, yet disaster and hardship arrived often.

Roads from the N2 to villages like Ndzongiseni were untarred, rarely traversed by cars, and constantly eroded by flash floods, summer thunderstorms, and overgrazing. The makeshift paths were worn into mini dongas, long and deep gullies caused by soil erosion. These dongas were a consequence of too many livestock grazing on the same piece of land, worsened by occasional droughts that prompted prayers from the community for divine intervention.

It was in Ndzongiseni that I learned the meaning of the popular expression, 'Ushayina ngathi uyocela imvula' – your face is so shiny, it's as if you are going to ask for rain. I'd gone with Gogo Ma'am to an all-night vigil at a makeshift church, where the community was gathering to pray for rain. Gogo Ma'am had smeared my face with a thick layer of Vaseline for the cold.

When rain failed to come, the livestock grew thin and frail.

The cattle's gaunt ribs protruded as they searched for water and grass. At times, when we would wander along the dry riverbed, we'd come across a carcass of a cow being devoured by giant vultures. The stench was intense. The vultures were unafraid of people, and they'd carry on eating as we walked past them.

When it rained, crossing the rivers in Ndzongiseni was another challenge. This was not a feat for the brave, but for the foolish. There were no bridges, so people would wait by the banks until the dirty brown waters subsided enough to wade through on foot or using vans (not the shoes, but bakkies).

Sometimes, the river would rise unexpectedly after a storm up on the mountain, and it was not uncommon to hear stories of someone being swept away by the river. If we didn't hear wailing after a thatched-roof hut had been struck by lightning during a storm, we hoped we wouldn't hear people screaming by the river, recovering someone who'd drowned. Fortunately for me, I was never in a position to witness someone drowning, but I had seen smoke rising from homes after a lightning strike.

Ndzongiseni's soil was a deep red, unlike the earth where I came from. When I asked the children who had grown up there why the soil was red, they explained that it was stained from many wars fought long ago. The surface layer was loose, made up of particles too big to be soil but too small to be pebbles. If you ran on it without dexterity, you would likely slip, slide and fall. But we kids were always barefoot, which gave us the best grip and traction, ensuring we didn't lose balance and fall.

In this landscape, every house was a traditional Xhosa mud-brick rondavel. The mud bricks were made on demand whenever a new home was being built, and once construction was complete, the woman would do the plastering by hand, called rhida, smoothing each brick into place with mud. After several days, when the mud had dried, the hut would be painted with a water-based paint called Ikalika in shades of white, powder blue, or powder pink.

Dutyini was poor, but Ndzongiseni was even poorer, more isolated from the flow of the outside world. There was only one car I saw regularly on the gravel road – a Datsun bakkie (which we called Bhotsotso), driven by a large white man who was probably the owner of the local general dealer. He always wore khaki shorts and a collared shirt, speeding down the long stretch of decent gravel road as if he couldn't wait to leave the place. The car was always followed by a large plume of dust, and when there was no wind, it would take some time for it to settle.

Many pedestrians used the side of the dirt road, but he wouldn't slow down when he saw anyone walking. People had to scatter out the way, their bags of groceries and supplies balanced on their heads. He'd let them eat dust, literally, as he sped past them.

'Usile lo mlungu!' people would mutter after he passed. This white man is ill-mannered and disrespectful! At the time, I didn't know what a racist was, but I could feel the disrespect in the way he drove as if the dirt roads of Ndzongiseni were his personal racetrack.

Apartheid had really done a number on the people on the outskirts, in places like Ndzongiseni. Villages in the so-called TBVC (Transkei, Bophuthatswana, Venda, and Ciskei) states were isolated from hospitals, schools, and basic conveniences, making success difficult to achieve.

The poverty in Transkei was deep and persistent. Life was hard and sometimes cruel – but for most, it simply was what it was, and everyone did the best they could, facing their hardships with humour and fortitude.

My childhood villain era

I don't recall the events I'm about to share, and actually, I'm glad I don't. They reveal a child who was calculating, vindictive, vengeful, and downright mean-spirited – or, depending on your perspective, a child with an extreme sense of duty and loyalty to his family. How you judge young Khaya in this story depends entirely on your worldview. Brace yourself: this tale is not merely petty – it's diabolical.

The events unfolded when I was around seven or eight years old in Dutyini, at my maternal grandparents' homestead. Makhulu told my mother this story, who, in turn, relayed it to me. Every time I hear it, I find it hard to believe that I could have done what I'm accused of. The decisions I supposedly made sound both impulsive and frighteningly calculated.

The target of my alleged villainy was a boy about a year or two older than me. He had been sent to Makhulu on an errand. Makhulu was renowned throughout the village for her generosity and kind-heartedness. If ever there was a model Christian in our community, she was the person most people would point to. Her home was a hive of activity, with villagers seeking her help for one thing or another.

The boy came to the gate, as visitors often did, calling out my name. It was a custom for guests to announce themselves at the gate, and as the youngest boy in the household, it was my duty to escort them in and protect them from our dogs, whose fearsome reputation was far greater than their actual bite.

'KHAYALETHU!' he called. Being the obedient grandchild I was raised to be, I went to the gate to open it and escort him inside.

Once in the kitchen, the boy was offered a cold jug of amarhewu to quench his thirst, a typical act of hospitality in our home. He downed it with the eagerness of a child, leaving a neat ring of the runny sour porridge around his mouth. Makhulu wiped his face, and asked me to rinse the jug and return it to the kitchen.

The boy had been sent to Makhulu by his mother asking for a favour: his mother wanted to borrow a cock. The poultry variety, you filthy-minded bastards.

She wanted to borrow one of Makhulu's roosters to, well, screw her lone hen so she could start her own brood of chickens. Makhulu had many chickens in the yard, so as expected, she agreed without hesitation. She instructed me to help the boy catch a rooster from the hen pen.

I led him to the yard, sprinkling chicken feed along the way to lure the flock into the pen. Once they were inside, I closed the gate to keep them contained while he chased a rooster around. After much flapping and squawking, he finally caught one, and we took it back to Makhulu for her approval. She gave her okay and I went back to open the gate. They were free to roam the yard again now that a sex slave had been selected.

As I walked the boy and the rooster to the gate, my inner villain allegedly emerged.

Life is like that sometimes

According to the tale, I turned to him and said, 'Do you remember when I walked past your house and you swore at me? You said you'd beat me up the next time you saw me. Well, this is next time.'

Instead of opening the gate, I set the dogs on him. Lion, Danger, Bhubesi, and Njencane sprang into action, barking ferociously. The boy screamed and fell to the ground in terror as the dogs surrounded him, barking wildly. Despite their terrifying reputation, the dogs didn't harm him – they simply barked and made a show of their presence.

Makhulu heard the commotion and rushed outside, shouting, 'Voetsek!' to call off the dogs. She assumed I'd lost control of them. The rooster had long since escaped, and the boy, shaken and crying, was brought back to the house.

To make amends, Makhulu slaughtered a chicken, cooked it, and gave him a thigh to eat on his way home. She even told him to ask his mother to come back the next day to collect the rest of the cooked chicken. She was mortified that the dogs had seemingly attacked this poor child.

She made me walk him back to the gate, even though the dogs were tied up this time. Again, as the obedient, dutiful grandson, I did as I was told.

When I returned to the kitchen, Makhulu noticed chicken fat smeared across my face. Suspicious, she asked how it had come to be there.

Without missing a beat, I allegedly told her that the boy gave me his piece of chicken to eat. Touched by what she believed to be an act of kindness, Makhulu smiled and thought to herself, *What a kind and sweet boy he must be.* The next day, the boy returned with his mother. The woman laughed when she got to Makhulu. Her son had come home crying, she said.

'Shame, he was really shaken by those dogs. I am so sorry for that. Please accept my apology, my child.'

Makhulu apologised to the child and mother. The mother continued to laugh. 'He was not crying because of the dogs. He says umzukulu wakho [your grandson] grabbed his meat, ate it in front of him and handed him amathambo antlantlathiweyo [crushed chicken bones]. And,' she added, 'he also says it was your grandson who set the dogs on him!'

Now my gran was even more apologetic. Not only did she give her the chicken she'd cooked, she told her she could keep the rooster they had come to borrow.

When I returned later that day, Makhulu wasted no time interrogating me. 'Khayalethu, why did you do that to another child?' she asked, with both exasperation and curiosity.

Without hesitation, I replied, 'He swore at me when I walked past his house the other day. He said the reason my grandfather has so many cattle is because he's a thief and practises witchcraft. I was avenging his insult. He can't get away with saying that about Tat'omkhulu.'

At this, Makhulu couldn't help but laugh. 'Then why don't you help your grandfather with his witchcraft,' she said through her laughter, 'instead of setting dogs on other children?'

It was a lesson in justice as only a child could understand it: misguided, extreme, and unapologetically loyal.

Benches and operating on myself

If there was one thing my grandfather, Alfred Kaiser Boyce, taught me without outright saying so, it was to always be prepared. He was both stern and loving, tough yet gentle. He never taught through words but always through action, and because of that, no one could ever call him a hypocrite. His lessons were always 'do as I do'.

Tat'omkhulu used his hands often. When I think of him now, I picture him busy with his big ass and those wide, chunky hands. I may not be a big person, but my hands are larger than they should be for my size – chunky and soft. People sometimes comment on how soft they are, quickly following it up with accusations of never having done a single day of hard labour. Which, of course, is absolutely false. Not working with your hands when you are Alfred Kaiser Boyce's grandson? Impossible.

When I was a little boy, my job was to hold tools for him while he fixed various things around the large homestead. I was like a nurse in an operating theatre, paying attention and watching his hands, waiting for instructions. He was also an impatient man, and his instructions had to be obeyed swiftly. If he called for a nail, I was to pass it on quickly. Taking your time was not an option.

A number of my older male relatives had gone to work in the mines in Johannesburg (or eGoli, eRhawutini, or eJwanesbag, as they often called it). My aunts and older female cousins often remind me how, as a boy between the ages of five and eight, I would go into their homes wielding tools like hammers, nails, and pliers to 'fix' things.

To this day, when I visit Dutyini, a relative will remind me of how I'd show up to hammer down protruding nails on benches or fix wobbly doors, as early as six years old. I'd observed my grandfather doing the same around our home. He was industrious and had a knack for 'engineering' solutions to broken things, finding ways to fix them that others wouldn't think of. But he'd never call it engineering – he was simply finding a solution to a problem.

Just because he was injured didn't mean he couldn't work. One time he hurt his leg badly while planting a field, but he carried on, limping through the work. So when I grew three warts on my hand, the idea of going to a doctor didn't even cross my mind. There was no clinic to go to in the village, and I'd only ever heard of people going to hospital if they were on the verge of death, had broken a leg or an arm, or needed surgery. Of course, nowadays I have become significantly softer – I go see a doctor at the slightest inconvenience, and I am certain that my grandfather turns in his grave every time.

The warts weren't particularly sore, but they were irritating and impossible to ignore. They grew on my left palm, feeling like grainy, rough bumps on the fleshy base of my thumb. One day, I took a pair of nail clippers and decided to chop them off. I realised the warts had roots embedded in the muscles, so I started digging into the flesh, feeling the crunch of the clippers on the roots. If I could still hear the crunch, I figured, the roots could still grow.

Tat'omkhulu was tough, and I could be too. I kept cutting, despite the blood that was now oozing out and making it difficult for me to see clearly. I poured water over the bleeding wound to see the roots more clearly. I dug around with the clippers until I removed every last bit. When I look at my left palm today, I sometimes think I can still see faint scars from where I operated on myself.

I bandaged my hand with an old shirt and got on with life, performing whatever chaos I had to perform, never complaining and never explaining.

Of course, I'm not as tough as that child was, though, for reasons I can't explain. I've become squeamish in my old age and soft with the comforts of Western medicine. The thought of a needle in my flesh is bound to solicit over-reactions from me these days. Yet when I was younger, I could face anything with the same resilience my grandfather showed in every situation.

Unganyabi!

It was not unusual to hear my mother say, 'Andimfuni umntwana onyabileyo' ('I don't want a dull, lifeless child'). To her, dullness made you vulnerable to being gobbled up and spat out by those who know how to assert themselves. Rather than being dominated or overlooked, you needed personality and presence in the world.

She believed that no child was born dull. It was circumstances – household environments or unchallenged fears – that dulled them. My mother made it her mission to root out any trace of dullness in the children she raised, moulding them into individuals who could project confidence and command respect.

Her own voice wasn't loud or aggressive, but it carried conviction. She believed you didn't have to shout to be assertive and make yourself heard. A voice, even when soft, should project confidence and presence. It should not sound as if it's hiding.

Ukunyaba goes beyond any simple translation, but it is an isiXhosa word that no child ever wants to hear applied to them. In fact, the term is not so much *said* as expelled: Unyabile! Sunyaba! Akanyabe! (You are dull! Stop being dull!) The words sting, not just for the moment but for the lasting impression they leave. This is one of the reasons many Xhosa people are known for being extroverted: they are raised to avoid the label of ukunyaba at all costs.

In fact, a lot of people confuse ukunyaba with introversion, but they are not the same. Introverts can be, and often are, very strong-willed and capable of standing up for themselves. They cannot be messed around with.

To be meek in isiXhosa is ubulali, a quality that might even be considered virtuous in some contexts, as Psalm 37:11 in English reads: 'But the meek will inherit the land and enjoy peace and prosperity.'³ In isiXhosa, Iindumiso 37:11 states: 'Ke bona abalulamileyo baya kulidla ilifa lelizwe ...'⁴ But while 'abalulamileyo' refers to meekness as a virtue, ukunyaba goes much deeper, describing a dull, lifeless demeanour that is far from admirable.

Unlike meekness or introversion, ukunyaba means to be uninspiring, lethargic, unable to stand up for oneself, and generally lacking in presence. It's the kind of label that can cling to you, shaping how others see you and how you see yourself.

This is why my mother waged a one-woman war against ukunyaba. To her, it was unacceptable. She taught me that meekness isn't the same as humility, and introversion doesn't mean a lack of agency. What mattered to her was that I would never let the world assume I was invisible or insignificant.

I've written before about how, when I was a young boy, she'd dress me in a suit, drape my jacket over my finger like a businessman, and send me off to talk to teachers as though I was negotiating a merger. I'd swagger up to them, hand in my pocket, and say, 'xolo, sis, ndicela ukuthetha nawe. Khawuz' apha.' ('Excuse me, sisi, I want to talk to you. Please come here.') The teachers, of course, would laugh when they realised this pint-sized Casanova was just a child.

When I started learning English, she made me approach white children. 'Because one day you will work with them,' she'd say, 'and I don't want you being scared of white people.' She was preparing me for a world that didn't always welcome us, making sure I'd never shrink back when it was time to take my place in it.

My mother knew that confidence was not innate but nurtured. She worked tirelessly to ensure her children were never dulled by circumstance. When my mother believed a child to be a member of the nyabile class, she made sure to push them. She'd send the child on various errands at a quick pace and urge them, 'Suyekelela umzimba man!' ('Do not let your body ebb energy away!') She encouraged quick thinking, action, and speaking up.

While her lessons were often disguised as playful challenges, in hindsight, they were her way of preparing me for a world that can easily disregard those who don't assert themselves.

Many years later, I found myself in a corporate office, working under a tough, highly intelligent woman. She had a formidable presence that made people pace nervously in the hallway before knocking on her door. There was a sense of trepidation around her, and while it kept everyone on their toes, it also fuelled a level of fear.

One day, I found myself in her office with a direct report. She was livid about a decision I'd made without consulting her. I explained that I had emailed, texted, and called her but couldn't reach her. I had no choice but to act. The decision couldn't wait – a delay would have cost the company R4 million.

Life is like that sometimes

She wasn't satisfied. Furious, she began shouting – not just at me, but at my colleague too. No one had ever shouted at me at work before. Ever. I felt something rise in me. I looked her in the eye and said, 'You should direct your dissatisfaction at me, not at him. I approved the other decision too.'

Her voice got louder, and the tension in the room became unbearable. That's when I interrupted her firmly, 'You might think what I'm about to say is rude or disrespectful, but I'm going to ask you not to talk to me that way. Here's what I'm going to do: I'm going to walk out of this office before either of us says something we can't take back. Please know that me walking out is not an act of rudeness – it's for both our sakes. When I come back, I expect us to have a conversation as adults.'

And with that, I walked out.

The second the door closed behind me, regret and fear crashed over me. *What have I done? I've made myself a target. I could get fired for this. What was I thinking? Oh Lord, help me! Seriously? Did I really say I expect us to have a conversation as adults? Wow!* I paced up and down the hallway, trying to calm down. After about five minutes, I walked back into her office.

When I returned, the atmosphere was awkwardly still. She was staring down at her desk, and my colleague was sitting on the couch, eyes fixed on the floor. I took a deep breath and said, 'I'm back now. I think we can have a conversation.'

This time, the shouting was gone. We talked, listened, and ultimately reached an understanding.

During our next one-on-one meeting, she surprised me. 'I'd like your feedback. How am I doing as a leader? How can I get better?'

One of the first things I told her was that people were afraid of walking into her office. She had no idea. It was a turning point. I saw her make a conscious effort to evolve, to become a leader who no longer wanted to be feared but respected.

My mother's determination to root out any trace of ukunyaba in me is one that has stayed with me and shaped how I approach the world: presence matters. But through her guidance, I also came to understand that presence doesn't mean being loud, overbearing or domineering. It means showing up with confidence, clarity, and a sense of self-worth – knowing when to speak and how to stand your ground, even if, like me, your voice is soft or your stature small.

Avoiding ukunyaba is not just about projecting energy or charm and avoiding ridicule or discomfort. It's about living deliberately, carrying yourself with a quiet assurance that your voice matters, your actions carry weight, and your presence has the power to shift a room.

Too much fighting in cities for me

After the passing of our father, our mother became determined to give us experiences. She often took us on holidays, perhaps as a way of dealing with her own sadness. She only saw us about once a month and during school holidays, so these trips were a way for her to connect with us. One of her favourite places was the Wild Coast, a beautiful but rugged 250-kilometre stretch along the east coast of South Africa, between the Mtamvuna River near KwaZulu-Natal and the Great Kei River in the Eastern Cape.

Though my sister and I never felt abandoned, our mother couldn't escape the guilt that many mothers feel when they have to be away from their children for long periods, even when they have little choice. She once told us that mothers feel guilty even if they're in a hospital bed on the verge of death.

On one of these trips, we stayed at one of Sol Kerzner's hotels in Mzamba. Kerzner, a South African hotelier, had found a way to sidestep the apartheid government's gambling laws by building casinos in the former TBVC states, where gambling was legal. The white population flocked to the neighbouring 'states' to gamble and enjoy the relaxed segregation rules, which made places like Mzamba especially popular.

One morning, my mother woke my sister and me at 6 am and suggested we catch a bus to the beach. Somewhere along the way, we stopped at a large dam and stumbled upon a sight that blew our village-born minds. There, on the water, a white man in a bright orange life jacket was being pulled behind a speeding boat. He was gripping a long rope as he zipped across the surface of the water, twisting and turning. I ran along the dam's edge, amazed each time someone took their turn being pulled across the water.

As exciting as it was to watch the skiing, the novelty wore off quickly. We were only spectators, not participants in this magical spectacle of gliding across the dam on our feet. My mother must have noticed.

Afterwards, we caught another bus to get to the beach, where we noticed locals selling what I now believe were crayfish. We hadn't been there long when a commotion broke out. A local woman was selling crayfish, and a heated argument erupted between an Indian man and a white man over who had the right to buy first. The Indian man had arrived maybe 30 seconds before the white man, so we saw him first and figured he'd be served first.

As the local woman held up one of the large red crustaceans from a bucket, I asked my mother what they were. I was familiar with crabs, as we often caught and released them by the river in Dutyini while herding sheep or cattle. The goal here was to see who would be the fastest to catch a crab or who would get the biggest crab.

'It's crayfish,' she answered. 'It's like crab but not the same. People with money pay a lot for it – but here, people who live in this area, who live in those rondavels, just catch it and eat it for free.'

'Sies! Batya le nto? ('Gross! They eat that thing?') my sister and I exclaimed, appalled at the idea. 'Kanti banjani abelungu?' ('Why on earth are white people like this though?')

My mother laughed and told us that they actually eat crayfish all around the world and that it's a sign of wealth because they were so expensive. 'One of those could cost an entire grocery bill.'

We were beyond flabbergasted.

As the argument between the white man and the Indian man escalated, we might as well have been watching a movie and eating popcorn. My mother was busy translating for us because we could not speak English.

She said, 'Bayathukana.' ('They are swearing at each other.') She wouldn't share exactly what they were saying. 'Ithi le ndoda yeNdiya akukho South Afrika apha, kuseTranskei, akanakuvela nje athenge kuqala ngenxa yokuba engumlungu.' ('The Indian man is telling the white man that this is not South Africa – it is Transkei. He can't just budge in and buy first if there are black people in line.')

I didn't really understand what she meant by that, but I did know that white people had much nicer things than other races.

'Hayibo! EliNdiya lithi lizakubulala lendoda yomlungu!' ('No way! The Indian man just told the white man that he is going to kill him!')

'Uzombulalela le nto? Bebadala kangaka?' ('Just for that thing? And these people are so old!')

The white man grabbed cash from his bag, shoving it at the woman as if to settle the dispute. Then all sorts of hell broke loose. The Indian man, fuming, lunged at him, grabbing his shirt. A wrestling match began.

The crayfish seller tried to separate them, pleading that if they kept fighting, the casino might ban all crayfish sellers and this is their livelihood. The next thing we saw, the woman was shoved aside by the men and she fell to the ground.

I don't recall how the fight ended but the white man was still on the ground when the Indian man paid and took his crayfish.

I turned to my mother, sharing my unhappiness about the situation. This whole thing was her fault.

'Kanti anti kutheni usisa kwiindawo kuliwayo kuzo? Wasisa eDurban nakhona kwakusiliwa.' I asked her why she always takes us to places where there is fighting. There had been fighting when she took us to Durban too.

I could not understand her choices. A few months earlier, she had taken us to the beach in Durban. While I was swimming, I heard people screaming and scattering. I saw police firing teargas into the crowd.

I tried to find my sister and cousins on the shore where I'd left them, but they were nowhere to be seen. I wandered aimlessly, tears streaming down my face. The teargas made it hard to see where I was supposed to go, and the chaos of people running added to my disorientation.

Crying and running, I felt a hand grab my arm and I tried to fight it off. Not only was I lost – now I was also being stolen.

'Ndim, Khayalethu.' ('It's me, Khayalethu.')

It was my aunt, Thobeka Dandala's mother. I continued to cry while she carried me to the minibus we had hired from Pietermaritzburg, covering our faces with a wet towel to protect us from the teargas.

Now, just a few months later, we had witnessed another fight at the beach. 'Don't take us this side again because they are always fighting here. No way. I'd rather you take us where you stay in East London because there is no fighting there when we are at the beach. Or you can just leave us in Dutyini,' I said to my mother, then, wondering aloud: 'Kanti kunjani nje ezidolophini?' ('Is this the way it is in the cities?')

She laughed gently and tried to explain a concept I didn't yet understand. She told me that people had been fighting on the Durban beach that day for a reason – they were fighting for their freedom, for the right to be anywhere in the country without restriction.

She then explained that that Indian man was not crazy. Not too far away from where we were in the Transkei was South Africa; there, that white man would have been allowed to push ahead of black people and buy first.

I could not understand. 'Even if he is not old and frail? He can just buy ahead of everybody just because he is white?'

Back in Dutyini and Mount Ayliff, we let old people buy ahead of us all the time. It was a social rule we all knew. Sometimes they would wait outside the shop and ask a younger person to buy for them.

My mother then shared a terrible event she had witnessed. She told us that a few years back, a prominent civil rights lawyer named Griffiths Mxenge was killed in King Williams Town for fighting to free black people.

She'd attended the funeral, where thousands of people had sung freedom songs and toyi-toyi'd. When a policeman appeared, the crowd grabbed him and began to beat him before setting him on fire.

While I did not fully comprehend the meaning behind what my mother was telling me, I was captivated by the sheer brutality of the story she was sharing. Why would a crowd just randomly kill a cop? I couldn't wrap my young mind around it. But as she spoke, something in her words began to shift my perspective. Slowly, she was pulling back the curtain, revealing the cruelty and injustice of the system that was apartheid.

Up until that point, I had thought the fights and chaos I'd witnessed were just random, messy clashes that were often at the expense of me having fun – like that time I'd been swimming in Durban, and now, grown men fighting over things that looked like crabs.

Yet, my mother's words hinted at something far deeper. These were battles being fought – not petty squabbles, but battles for dignity, fairness, and freedom. Still, as much as I tried, I couldn't fully comprehend the weight of what she was trying to tell me.

In many ways, growing up in Dutyini shielded me from the harsh realities of apartheid, even though, ironically, the very reason we lived in such an impoverished village was because of that very same system. The land we called home, the simplicity of our lives, the lack of access to opportunities – it was all shaped by the same oppressive force my mother was beginning to make me aware of.

The girl who wore the pants

Growing up in a rural community comes with a set of spoken and unspoken rules that shape the society. Many are conservative, intended to establish order and a sense of hierarchy. Manners and politeness were important and expected – not only from each other but especially so from children when interacting with adults. The sense of familiarity or overly comfortable behaviour from children around adults was unheard of in Dutyini.

Where I grew up, adults were treated with deference, reverence and respect, and children were expected to show politeness and restraint, especially around their elders. Any adult could discipline an ill-mannered child. It really did take a village to raise a child then.

One rule, for example, set how children greeted adults. A child had to use both hands to shake an adult's hand – either cupping it respectfully or lightly grasping their right wrist with their left hand as a sign of good manners and humility. We were also taught never to look an adult in the eye when greeting them; it was a symbol of reverence and sound character.

Of course, another sign of good morals was avoiding

drinking or smoking. But worse than drinking or smoking was a woman who wore pants. There could be no worse demonstration of a woman's moral failings. The only thing worse than a woman who wore pants was a woman who wore pants *and* smoked *and* drank. To the people of Dutyini, such a woman was beyond redemption. They looked at her not only with disgust and disapproval but with a great deal of pity, certain that hell awaited her in the next life.

When I was growing up, I never saw a woman in Dutyini wearing pants, but I had seen plenty who drank traditional beer. The only exception was my mother, and that was when she rode my grandfather's horse to a neighbouring village. And even then, it was not just the pants that were unprecedented – it was the fact that she, as a woman, was riding a horse at all. I tell this story in *To Quote Myself* – how the whole village came to a standstill when they saw her on a horse.

My mother was a rebel without intending to be one. She simply wanted to do what made her happy, as long as it caused no harm. Growing up in rural Transkei, she had little access to fashion, yet she loved good clothes. This was unexpected for someone who was, in many ways, a tomboy.

From a young age, she took care of her father's cattle in the veld alongside other village boys and girls. She climbed trees, swam in the river, learned stick fighting – whatever the boys did, she could do too. She was a tomboy with a secret love for fashion.

Magazines were hard to come by in the village, but when she saw one, she'd keep it, hiding it so that no one would use its pages as toilet paper. She would look at the images of clean, beautiful women and imagine herself as one of them. She didn't want to be out looking after cattle in the field. She wanted to be glamorous.

She had two older sisters, Nomakhosi and Nolulama Boyce. Nomakhosi lived in Durban with my grandmother's sister, who worked as a domestic for a white family. Whenever Nomakhosi came home to visit, she brought magazines and catalogues for her younger sisters. With whatever money she had, my mother would save to buy clothes from a catalogue. This was their version of online shopping back then – ordering clothes and not even knowing if they would fit.

Whenever my grandfather sent her to town, she would secretly pack her fashionable clothes, hiding them in a plastic bag behind the kraal the night before. She'd leave home in a normal dress, carrying her fashionista outfit in the plastic bag, and make her way to town. When she got there, she'd head to the Catholic Church, change into her fancy clothes, and find a photographer to take pictures of her in pants. Once she was done, she'd switch back to her average dress before returning home because a girl wearing pants was still a big no-no.

Basically, she had her own Instagram account that nobody could see and without the likes.

Her secret actions were a fight for the woman she wanted to be. It wasn't loud or confrontational, but quiet and deliberate – a defiance rooted in self-assurance. In every photograph, she could freeze time and preserve a vision of herself. It was her way of making a statement, saying: *This is who I am – and one day, the world I live in will catch up.*

Losing my grandmother

I was an entirely restless child who possessed all the deceptive appearances of innocence when I was around adults. I was quick to obey grown-ups and well-mannered in their midst – but a self-trained rascal when I was nowhere near adults.

While my sister and I lived with our grandparents in Dutyini, my mother lived in Mdantsane, about 500 kilometres away. Even from that distance, she could sense that my life was at a crossroads, especially after we lost my grandmother, Vuyelwa, when I was eight years old.

My mother only visited us a couple of times a month, and she had no idea that I had become a weed-smoking, class-bunking eight-year-old hoodlum, but she sensed that something wasn't right.

My grandfather, once a towering figure of discipline and strength, was a shadow of his former self after losing his wife. The heartbreak had drained the authority from his voice.

There is a photo my mother once sent me of him at the funeral. He is reaching into the pocket of his oversized black suit, his grief-stricken face looking downwards. The few village women visible in the image are wrapped in shawls and their faces also speak the language of loss.

I asked my mother if he was reaching for a handkerchief inside the jacket. She told me that he was reaching for a letter that he had written to his wife. He simply placed the letter inside the open casket and went back to sit down. Nobody knows what he wrote in the letter, but the heartbreak in his face was apparent. It was the kind of heartbreak that makes you look away when the person wearing it looks at you.

My mother often spoke of the deep respect my grandfather had for my grandmother and how much he had loved her. She was the love of his life and then she was gone. It was easy to see how much he adored her.

That heartbreak didn't just change him – it changed everything. Before losing Makhulu, the mere thought of bunking school would have sent me straight to my grandfather to confess. But now, with his spirit blunted by grief, I unknowingly became a law unto myself. Perhaps, in my own reckless way, this was how I processed the loss of my gentle, kind grandmother – by letting the structure she had anchored in our lives quietly unravel.

Grief has a way of sneaking up on you, especially when you're too young to name it or know it. It reshapes you before you even notice what's happening. I had lost my father at six, then my uncles in a tragic accident at seven, and now, at eight years old, my grandmother – a woman I saw and spent time with almost every single day.

I had spent more time with her than with the mother who birthed me. Losing her felt like losing a part of myself. She was also the only person who could protect me from my grandfather's strictness. But now, even my grandfather had suddenly become invisible in the home his presence once loomed over.

At the time, I didn't even know what grief was, let alone that I was handling it like an amateur. Not that anyone can deal with it like a pro. I was an eight-year-old muddling through a loss I couldn't fully understand, and my response was rebellion masquerading as freedom, skipping school, and smoking weed.

My primary school underworld operation

After the passing of my grandmother, my mother decided to remove me from the village school in Dutyini, where I'd been for a couple of years after Gogo Ma'am's school. My mother could see a future that would leave me stuck in one place. Village life has a way of suffocating dreams, or even the possibility of having them. Being taken out of the village would show me that the world was bigger and had a space for me to dream beyond it.

I arrived at Little Flower Junior Secondary School, a Catholic boarding school, with the tendencies of an outlaw and rebel. Life in the village may have given me a sense of hopelessness, and the passing of my grandmother a few months before had affected me more than I realised. I had no idea I was about to become a mastermind in the primary school black market.

At Little Flower, we not only had to bring our own clothes but also bedding and supplies, including toilet paper. Each child brought twelve toilet rolls, stored in a communal storeroom. To preserve this commodity, we were instructed to use precisely four squares of toilet paper at a time. No one policed us, yet we all did as we were told.

I secured a top bunk bed as I had arrived two days early along with my older cousins Nobulali and Unathi Mshumi, veterans in their final year at the school. My mother and aunt thought this early arrival would help them show me the ropes.

I didn't mind at all – I had never seen such a fancy school in my life. The road from the N2 to the school was tarred, the classrooms had electricity, and there were beds and even showers.

This was a five-star hotel compared to Dutyini. It was probably the first time I had ever seen a shower. There was indoor plumbing. Not a single classroom had a broken window. Not one. The grass was immaculate; there were roses and large trees. I thought I had stepped into a palace.

Years later my mother told me how devastated she was when she left me there by myself. But I was thrilled to be in such a cushy environment. No more herding cattle or fetching water from the river. To me, this was paradise.

One of the items I brought with me was a pillow. My mother had got me a soft one, wanting me to have the same comforts as the other kids, and perhaps to ensure that no one teased me or looked down on me because I came from a village. Because of that, my confidence never took a knock. I didn't know what it meant to be rich or poor, only that I was the same as other kids.

I'd never used a pillow in my life. Back home in Dutyini, I either slept on a mattress on the floor with my cousins in a rondavel, or shared a room with my uncle who seemed to be having sex every night with women of various shapes and sizes when he thought I was asleep. I was too young to know what sex was, but the moans and screams and giggles, accompanied by bedsprings making noises, was utterly confusing.

The only real purpose my pillow served for me was for the boy who slept below me on the bunk bed. His snoring had all the markings of an old man who had lived a long life and drunk heavily. He was a young, athletic, muscular boy, but his snoring was like that of a man who had lived through colonialism and apartheid – ancient and weary. I'd use the pillow to smack him to stop him from disturbing the peace. Strangely, the boys in the beds beside him never tried to wake him, now that I think about it.

I first ventured into the primary school criminal underworld when I noticed that the other kids loved my spongey pillow. They all complimented me on how soft it was. Maybe it was a reminder of the safety and tenderness of home. I didn't know, nor did I care – I was making money.

Every night, kids would come up to my bed to negotiate the use of my pillow. Before I saw the gap in the market, I'd lend it to whoever asked first. Then, like any savvy entrepreneur, I saw an opportunity.

After their free trial period, I started charging 10 cents a night on a first-come, first-served basis. They had to pay cash upfront. Since we weren't allowed to have money at the school, this made the whole operation technically illegal – but business boomed.

Strangely enough, even though money was banned and as extension, commerce was banned, there was always money floating around. The pillow scheme was the most profitable of ventures.

Thanks to my newfound wealth from this successful criminal enterprise, I also became a loan shark. One day, someone stole my money.

The other kids tracked down the thief and made him confess. If my money was gone, they couldn't borrow from me, so it was in their best interests to recover it.

I spent three years at that boarding school, and not once did anyone snitch. They got their soft nights, and I got to keep my soft life.

Stabbings in the village

I was about eleven years old, home for the school holidays from boarding school, when I heard that there had been a sudden spate of stabbings in Dutyini. A young man, in his late teens or early twenties, had begun attacking people with a knife at the slightest or even imagined provocation. People feared him, but there were no local police to report him to. The nearest police station was 15 kilometres away, in town, and there were no phones to call for help. Since no one had died or been critically injured, the villagers saw no reason to involve the police, who would take a long time to attend to the case anyway, given the wide area they covered.

The stabbings took place not too far away from Gogo Ma'am's house, near the junction used as a bus and minibus taxi stop. After a series of incidents, the villagers of Dutyini decided something had to be done. That *something* involved Tat'omkhulu.

A group was sent to Tat'omkhulu to report the stabbings and urge him to take action. When he heard what had been happening, he asked for a group of strong young men to meet him at his home that evening. They gathered in the rondavel, and he explained what he had been told about the stabbings at the junction and how unsafe people were feeling.

He gave them a task. They were to go apprehend the young man and bring him back to him. The next morning, a group of about six young men armed with fighting sticks ventured up towards the steep part of the village where the young man lived. They reached his family home while he was there, before breakfast. They explained to his parents that they had been sent to apprehend him because he had been identified by all the victims as the culprit. Surrounded by the young men, there was nowhere for him to run, and he was handed over.

They brought him to Tat'omkhulu, who was sitting in the tall, empty zinc shed that had been used to house a tractor years before. He wore his blue overalls and heavy brown work boots. The morning was already hot by the time they arrived. Tat'omkhulu took out his handkerchief, wiped his face, and put it back in his pocket.

'Do you know why they brought you to me?' he asked.

The young man feigned ignorance.

'Are you sure?' Tat'omkhulu said to him. 'Didn't they tell you?' His eyes narrowed. 'So you just agreed to come without knowing why?'

The young man remained silent.

'What did they say to you when they picked you up?' he asked.

'They said I stabbed people,' the young man muttered.

'Are you stabbing people?'

He denied it.

'So every single person who said you stabbed them is lying?' Tat'omkhulu's voice was stern. He asked the group of men to search his pockets, and they found a knife.

'What's this knife for?' the young man was asked.

He remained silent.

'What makes you think it's for you to stab people who haven't done anything to you?' my grandfather asked. 'What are you doing carrying a knife in the village? Do you think this a township?'

When Tat'omkhulu compared someone's behaviour to that of a person raised in a township, it was the biggest insult he could hurl at them. Tat'omkhulu had a deep disdain for the townships, believing that townships were where values went to die. To him, township life led to the decay of manners and common decency as people lived too close together and didn't have places to plough mealies or rear livestock. The presence of knives used for stabbings in the village was a sign of township mentality encroaching on traditional values – the beginning of the end for him. He would do anything he could to stop it.

'I am going to remove this township mentality you have.' He ordered the young men to take the boy to a hut that was furthest from all the other buildings in the homestead. This rondavel stored animal feed, a grinding stone for dry mealies, as well as his saddles, tools, sjamboks and whips. He told them to tie him to the wooden pillar at the centre of the rondavel.

'I am going to beat the lokishi out of you.'

After ensuring the boy was securely tied, he told the young men to go to the kitchen for food and thanked them for their work. He walked with them to the kitchen, leaving the boy tied up alone in the rondavel.

When the young men had finished eating, Tat'omkhulu dismissed them, saying he would deal with the stabber by himself.

Around lunchtime, my cousin Qiqa Mshumi, was sent to bring Tat'omkhulu his meal. As she approached the rondavel, she could hear whimpering from inside. The door was closed and locked. She knocked and called out that she had brought lunch.

'Kulungile mzukulu.' ('Thank you, my grandchild.')

He stepped out, wiping blood from his hands with a cloth, a whip still in his grasp. Qiqa placed the food tray on a bench in the shade nearby.

'Mzukulu, ask them to dish up for him too, and bring him amarhewu for him to drink,' he said.

He went back inside, untied the boy, and let him sit with him on the bench. The young man was teary-eyed, with the marks of lashes on his back.

The boy never stabbed anyone else in the village again. He became a model citizen, got married and moved to Johannesburg with his wife.

Moving to Mdantsane

Mdantsane was a world apart from the tranquillity and slowness of Dutyini village. Visiting the enormous township during school holidays always felt like exciting little adventures: I could dip my toes into township life before retreating to the comfort of the village. To me, the township was a technological giant leap compared to Dutyini. For one thing, I could go to the toilet inside a house. Day and night. It was like living in a science fiction movie.

My time in Mdantsane had always been limited to two-week school holiday visits at best. Even while attending Little Flower Junior Secondary School in Qumbu, my school breaks were divided between Dutyini, Danti, and Mdantsane. Each place felt like its own little world, and Mdantsane, because I never stayed long enough, carried that strange mix of familiarity and foreignness, like a relative you only see at funerals and weddings.

The house in NU 3 was my mother's house, but it did not feel like home as much as Dutyini did. (NU stands for Native Unit, a vestige from the apartheid government. Further down in the Western Cape, in Gugulethu, they are called NY for Native Yard.)

Of course, I was fascinated by the streetlights – something that we did not have in Dutyini – and the tap at the back of the house. It was a relief not having to grab a wheelbarrow to fetch water from the river. There was also a flushing toilet inside the house.

My mother lived in a typical four-room Mdantsane house. However, she did not have the whole house to herself. It was just two rooms, but she made those rooms work.

The main room had the sole purpose of being her bedroom (and her bathroom because she would bath there in a waskom). The other room was a multi-functional marvel: kitchen by morning, bedroom by night, visitor reception when someone came round, bathroom when it was time to wash in the mornings, and lounge in the rare moments we pretended to relax.

When I visited, it was my room. When I moved to Mdanstane, it was still my room, though the spoons, stove, and kitchen chairs would beg to differ.

On the other side of this four-room house lived a family of three: a woman and her two kids. Her commitment to being the grumpy neighbour was remarkable. Her face looked like she woke up every morning, stood in front of a mirror, and practised her scowl.

We shared a toilet inside the house with the other family. To be fair, they definitely drew the shorter straw in this arrangement. For us, getting to the toilet meant parading through their part of the passage in their part of the house. They, by contrast, had no access to our side.

The whole thing was terribly awkward, especially for them, I imagine. The door that led to the toilet opened directly into their passage, so every trip to the loo was an exercise in

Life is like that sometimes

hope: hope that no one was lurking, or that you didn't smack a housemate in the face if you opened the toilet door too quickly. But honestly, they had it worse – never knowing when someone from another family would emerge from behind a door in their space.

The house didn't have electricity, but our neighbour, Nonesi, was the real MVP. She let us store anything that needed refrigeration in her fridge. My sister and I regularly strolled over, knocked on her door, and sheepishly asked for whatever we'd parked there.

Sis' Joyce, an elderly woman who had taken a liking to me and was friends with my mother, lived in a house directly opposite us. Her house was where I went to watch TV.

We also didn't have a phone, which turned Nonesi's house into our phone booth. Every phone call meant walking over and politely invading her space.

Like us, Nonesi shared her house with a family of four: a granny, her daughter Nolatsi, and two boys slightly older than me. The older boy, Nampi, was the granny's son. The other boy, Mandisi, was Nolatsi's son. They were just a few months apart.

I worked out that Nonesi and her mother must have been pregnant around the same time. I am pretty sure this was a massive neighbourhood scandal at the time. I can just imagine old ladies in the hood, whispering over their fences, teacups in hand, dissecting every detail of this neighbourhood soap opera.

When my mother finally moved me from Dutyini to live with her in Mdantsane, I joined a full house: my two sisters, Sikelelwa (Siki) and Sikulo (Siku), my little brother, Nganga (the last-born), and my mother's boyfriend, Donald Tununu Gwiba.

I was twelve years old, had no friends, and, to be honest,

was perfectly fine with that. I had no interest in growing up to become a tsotsi, which is what my grandfather believed would happen to me if I lived in the township at such a young age. I carried my grandparents' voices with me, a reminder to hold on to the values that would guide me, no matter where I lived.

The textbook terrorists

I often sat on the front stoep after school and on weekends to watch the neighbourhood boys walking around the neighbourhood in groups. Their aimless wandering reminded me of what we did in the village, though in Mdantsane, the smaller yards meant kids played in the streets and had to make way for the occasional car.

When I moved, I thought my bicycle had been left behind in the village, a casualty of the transition. We lived in two rooms – of course, I figured there was no space for it. But one weekend, my mother revealed she'd been storing it in the ceiling, her own secret storage solution. Just like that, I was riding the streets of Mdantsane. I knew this was going to make me cool. I was right.

The neighbourhood boys quickly took notice, starting random conversations with me in the streets. Once again, a bicycle proved to be the ultimate social currency. Just as I'd been the only boy with a bike in Dutyini, I now held that title across several streets in NU 3 in Mdantsane.

Just as in Dutyini, a business opportunity soon presented itself. I started charging the neighbourhood boys to ride the bike. Of course, this enterprise only operated under strict conditions – namely, when my mother was not around. She would have been furious if she'd caught me letting strangers ride the bicycle she'd worked so hard to buy for me. In many ways, it was not just a bicycle – it was a symbol of her sacrifices.

My business venture came to an abrupt halt when the chain snapped for the final time.

Around the same time, I had neighbours who were a couple of years older than me. Mandisi, one of the boys, became more friendly as time went by. He'd start small talk and ask me what it was like going to school with white people. I was the only child in the neighbourhood, possibly for kilometres, who went to a white school. After Nelson Mandela's release, the white schools had voted to allow black kids, and I was part of that first batch.

One day, Mandisi approached me with something urgent to share.

'The boys in the neighbourhood know that you go to a white school in town, nhe?'

'Okay.'

'They said they are going to come over and ask to see your textbooks. They will say they want see if the textbooks from white schools and black schools are the same.'

'Okay. I'm sure I can show them,' I said innocently. I was keen to make new friends.

'No. They actually just want to take the books and burn them,' he explained.

I stared at him, unsure whether to take him seriously. It made no sense. How could anyone think to do such a thing?

'They are going to ask you this afternoon,' he warned, walking away like a spy delivering classified intel.

The afternoon came and went with no sign of these alleged

book arsonists. Now I was mad at Mandisi for spreading malicious rumours.

But the following Saturday, a group of five boys entered my yard. I had just finished cutting the lawn and was perched on the red, polished stoep.

They greeted me politely, asked some questions about what it was like to go to a white school, and then one of them casually said, 'Can you show us your textbooks? We want to see if they're the same as ours.'

I was flabbergasted. Mandisi wasn't a liar after all.

Fortunately, I had already devised a plan – just in case. Now was the time for its implementation.

'We leave our textbooks in a locker at school. We don't take them with us. Why don't you guys bring me your textbooks from home and I'll tell you if they're the same?' I suggested. They had played checkers whereas I was playing chess, and now it was checkmate.

They looked at each other, completely thrown off. After a few moments of hesitation, they mumbled something about fetching their books and left. Decades later, I'm still waiting for them to bring me their textbooks.

The bicycle and the textbooks became symbols of who I was at that moment. The bike was a fleeting crown of childhood glory, granting me power and belonging – until the chain snapped. The textbooks were a reminder that I didn't quite fit, that I was straddling two worlds: the streets of Mdantsane and the formal classrooms of a white school. Together, they taught me that belonging is never simple and that strength is often built in the spaces where we feel most out of place.

My mixed bag of art teachers

I don't know where my affinity for art came from, but I'm glad I found it. The schools I attended in what was then the Transkei didn't offer art as a subject. In fact, it never even occurred to me that it could be something you could learn at school. So when I arrived at Hudson Park Primary School in 1991, after the white parents at the school had voted to allow black children to attend, I was shocked to find art as part of the curriculum. At first, art seemed like an unnecessary luxury – a frivolous waste of time.

I had no idea what to expect for my first class. The art classroom was colourful and whimsical, covered in drawings and paintings that were clearly created by very talented children. I was horrified. I felt completely ill-prepared for this classroom. Were we expected to paint and draw like that? How was this a subject and how did the teachers even mark it?

Our art teacher at Hudson Park Primary was an extremely beautiful woman and the only teacher in the whole school who wore very high heels. They made a distinct click-clack sound as she walked, and we always knew it was her approaching. It was as if she was announcing her imminent arrival, and the sound of her heels were an order for us to maintain decorum so that she didn't have to tell us to be quiet. She carried herself with the grace of a model.

She was friendly and eager to teach us various art techniques, but as enthusiastic as she was, I never got the sense that teaching was her destiny. She taught us for a short while but after she got married, we never saw her again.

When I got to high school at Hudson Park High School, I opted to take art because I was not a gifted accountant. While I was good at logic, mathematics became my arch-enemy. I kept maths and accounting at a healthy distance.

I fell in love with art history and after school, I would go to the community library in Vincent, poring over books about Greek architecture, the Ionic Order, Romanticism, Baroque, Cubism, Expressionism, and Impressionism. I realised that the books never featured anything about African art.

At home, I'd kneel on the floor of my mother and sister's room, in front of the dressing table, and practise drawing self-portraits with a pencil. Later on, I attempted to draw my left hand. My drawings were not particularly good or bad – but they were closer to bad than good.

Hudson Park High had two art teachers, and they were unlike my glamorous primary school teacher. One was a stern, perpetually displeased woman in her late forties with dull sandy hair streaked with grey. She seemed to have little care for fashion, and nothing in her demeanour gave the impression that she wanted to be teaching – unless, of course, she did an excellent job in concealing her enthusiasm.

Based on my experience in primary school, I had assumed all art teachers were kind and beautiful with a positive predisposition. But this teacher taught us with languid, almost disdainful authority, her voice high-pitched and sharp. She looked like she had never been happy.

The closest she came to enthusiasm was when she talked about the scandalous lives of the artists. Artists' scandals just seemed so juicy, and we'd all listen to her attentively because it was like hearing a breaking-news story live.

We had never heard her compliment a single person. Ever. Except once.

During a practical exam, she kept walking into our classroom and stopping to stare at the piece I was painting. After the fourth or fifth time, I got a little agitated and said, 'Miss, you keep staring at my painting and saying nothing. If you have something to say, just tell me so I can fix it or change it.'

She stood over my work, arms still folded, her eyes fixed on the canvas lying on the floor. That's how I preferred to paint – with the canvas on the floor. After a long pause, she finally spoke in her high-pitched voice, 'You are going to become a very good painter one day.'

The entire class froze. Several people gasped. That was the nicest thing she had ever said to anybody.

Then, just as abruptly, she walked out.

If we did not listen to her, or were late, or did not do our homework, she would threaten us by shouting, 'If you continue, I will kick you out of my class and you will be forced to take accountancy.' One student disobeyed her one too many times, and she did exactly that. Needless to say, I ran into him years later and he'd become an extremely successful accountant. He'd become a partner at one of South Africa's top auditing firms.

The second teacher, a man, was her polar opposite. Eccentric and brilliant, he taught art history entirely from memory, never referring to a textbook or writing on the blackboard. He knew artists' names, paintings, life stories, and all the relevant dates off the top of his head. I'd go to the library to confirm these details, and he was right every time.

During our art history lessons, he'd just walk around the class, arms folded. As he spoke, we'd be writing down notes furiously. When he mentioned a French artist, he'd pronounce the name with a perfect French accent. None of us knew French; it was not even offered at school.

He'd say something like, 'Ferdinand Victor Eugène Delacroix, was born in 1798,' and get irrationally angry if someone raised their hand to ask, 'Sir, how do you spell Delakra?' He'd spell it very fast, his extreme irritation apparent, and we'd all be too scared to ask him to repeat it. 'It's spelled D. E. L. A. C. R. O. I. X.,' immediately launching into the next fact before we had even finished writing the name down. After class, we'd all gather together to figure out the correct spelling, though I often confirmed them later at the library because we didn't have textbooks for the subject.

When he marked our tests, he'd write angry comments in the margins when we got something wrong. These were scrawled in red pen in his horrendous, difficult-to-read handwriting. After marking one of my papers he'd written, 'What the f*^k is this, you shark fin?'

His infamous irritation at having to repeat himself meant that we would often wait and see who would be brave enough to ask him to repeat something. Sometimes, no one raised a hand to ask him and this led to hilarious consequences.

On one occasion, during a test on American art, I wrote the title of a Jackson Pollock painting as *'Lamb in the Mist'*. I was confident about the painting, and I knew all sorts of facts about it. When I got my test back, there was a furious note from him. He wanted to know what *'Lamb in the Mist'* was because the Jackson Pollock painting that we had covered in class was *Lavender Mist*. These were the consequences of his refusal to repeat himself and now we were both suffering. Since I got everything else right, he forgave me and gave me full marks, but not without a few F-bombs scribbled in the margin.

Despite all this, he was actually highly approachable and popular – as long as you weren't asking him to repeat anything. He'd throw in the odd life lesson too. Once, I told him I had never been dumped (I didn't mention that I had also never had a girlfriend), while a friend of mine told him about a recent heartbreak. 'You haven't lived until you have been dumped,' he said.

It's funny to think back to my first encounter with art class, feeling utterly flummoxed by the concept of it all. I thought, *What kind of people turn doodling into a subject?* To my young, rural-Transkei-raised mind, it was a frivolous waste of time, a luxury that only white people could afford to indulge in.

But life has a way of humbling you and shifting your perspective. The boy who once thought art class was ridiculous is now a lover of art.

Now, when I walk into an art gallery or lose myself in a painting, I think of that boy sitting in an art class, trying to make sense of it all. And I smile. Because art, much like life itself, isn't always something you understand right away. Life is like that sometimes, I guess.

Saturday-ing

In most township households, Saturdays were not synonymous with leisure. They were days of intense physical activity for all children. Houses had to be spring-cleaned (no matter the season), lawns mowed, cars washed, windows polished, stoeps scrubbed, and washing done.

I must have been about fourteen years old, living in Mdantsane with my mother, her boyfriend, Tununu, and my siblings – Sikelelwa, Sikulo, and my now late youngest sibling, my brother, Nganga. Sikelelwa was twelve, Siku was almost four years old and Nganga almost two years old.

Saturdays in our household ran like a finely tuned machine. My mother, ever the commander of order, expected everything to be spotless and in its place. These were the weekly tests of just how well we could rise to her standards. If something wasn't done right, my mother made you do it over and over again until you got it right. No one was going to do it for you. She had time and patience. There was no back-chatting, no outward facial expressions demonstrating frustration or annoyance. We had to present the perfect picture of stoicism. While Saturdays for other kids were for loitering in malls, going to the movies, and hanging out with friends, they were not that for me. Saturdays were for doing everything I hated. I had to wake up early because my bedroom also served as the kitchen and lounge, where we'd sit or receive guests. I'd wake up, make my bed, and fold it away. It collapsed neatly into a wooden structure. The whole bed vanished into it, and it looked like a fixture for displaying vases and our battery-operated radio. A stranger would never even suspect that there was a bed concealed inside.

After washing in the waskom in our kitchen-bedroom-lounge, I'd carry it outside, opening the zinc door, walking down three red steps, taking two right turns, and throwing the water out by the back drain.

Once my stomach was fed, I had to do 'Saturday things', which were time-consuming and lonesome. Despite how repetitive, mind-numbing, and annoying they were, I have to admit, with great reluctance, that they were also therapeutic.

Of all the Saturday things, having to shine windows using an old newspaper was the worst. I was never able to get those damn windows to shine without leaving smudge lines. My mother would try to show me how it's done, but still, I could never get it right. She'd make me do it over and over again.

Then it was time to wash Tununu's car, a task I also hated. Back then, most boys my age would have done anything to wash a car because you were touching a dream. Washing a car made the dream of owning a car feel so much closer, even possible. There was no hosepipe to use. Rather, I had to fill a bucket with water at the back of the four-roomed house then walk back with a full bucket to the front of the house, where the Nissan Langley was parked.

The worst was on cold days when my hands felt like they'd

Life is like that sometimes

freeze off as I dipped a cloth in icy water. I would finish washing the tyres last, using black shoe polish to make them shine.

Not long after washing the car, it was time to battle the grass. With only a pair of garden shears, cutting grass was a laborious process. I had a specific technique: I'd bend my left leg up with my thigh against my chest, knee almost touching my chin, while my right leg bent with my knee on the ground, and my right buttock rested on my heel.

Each snip of the shears only cut a few blades of grass, so I developed a rapid, repetitive motion to cover more ground. After an hour, my hands would cramp up and I'd have to pause, letting them relax for a short period. My hands would start feeling tingly, even itchy.

When the garden shears were broken, I had to resort to using sheep-shearing scissors, which was an even worse hell. My hand cramped up more quickly, and it took longer to finish, as I could only use one hand at a time.

Because my mother's sister, Nolulama, and her husband, Senzangakhona Mshumi (known as Theo), only had girls – Nobulali, Unathi, Qiqa, and Malubekho – they would often 'borrow' me from my mother on certain weekends. I'd either walk an hour from NU 3 to NU 7 or head to Highway to catch a taxi.

I didn't mind going because they were the rich cousins. They lived in what is called 'Ezitandini' ('Stands') – not the typical four-room houses of the township, but bigger homes in a section reserved for those who were financially better off.

I'll admit it: I loved visiting. There was a TV, and I could watch it whenever I wanted. At home in NU 3, I had to go to a neighbour's house just to catch the news before heading back. They had electricity, and I could take a bath in a real bathtub instead of washing in a waskom with a little water. It's not a nice thing to say, but I liked it more there.

Looking back, I think my mother made us work on Saturdays not just to keep the house in order, but to keep us in order.

She knew the township could easily pull you into its whirlwind of distractions and shenanigans, and she wasn't about to let that happen to us. Saturdays were her way of teaching us that staying busy with constructive things wasn't just about chores – it was about discipline, about grounding yourself in who you are and where you come from. She believed that hard work had a way of shaping you, of keeping you from drifting too far from your values.

The shortcut I liked to take

It was one of those overcast Sunday mornings – a good day to make what people in the Eastern Cape call Bisto. In that part of the world, overcast didn't necessarily mean cold.

My wrists were still aching from yesterday's grass-cutting when my mother summoned with her soft voice that somehow carried authority, 'Khayalethu!' I knew my mother's various tones and I could tell from her voice, along with the sound of coins jangling in her hand, that I was going to be sent to some shop.

This particular Sunday morning, she handed me money to go buy mincemeat from the butchery in the always-busy Highway. Highway is not to be confused with an actual highway (in fact, there are no highways in Highway). Rather, Highway is a place – the busiest area in Mdantsane. You could argue it was one of the busiest places in all of the Eastern Cape. It was like Grand Central Station for Mdantsane's minibus taxis, with hundreds of them converging, picking up and dropping off tens of thousands of passengers each day.

There were stands where women were selling fresh vegetables, defeathered chickens, loaves of bread, fried sausages, and beef. One of my favourite stands was run by a lady who sold a quarter loaf of white bread with tomato, cheese, and fried egg. She was generous with the sprinkling of Aromat on the egg, a seasoning I didn't get at home, so if I had any extra cash, I'd buy myself a double breakfast.

Because Highway is a major transportation hub, there were numerous small businesses. And of course – what shall I call these people? *Informal opportunistic businessmen*, perhaps? The word tsotsi is so ... judgemental.

In fact, there was even a shop where you could buy pirated music on CDs or cassettes. You could give them the original of what you wanted, and they'd copy it for you. No big deal. I don't think anybody thought that it was a criminal enterprise, even the bootleggers themselves. We had no idea how the music publishing world worked. All we knew was that we paid money and then got a CD.

So, when my mother summoned me that Sunday morning, I was glad because I'd get to be outside the house for a while. I was always at home and had no friends in the neighbourhood.

She gave me loose change for the pack of mincemeat I was sent to buy, and I clutched the coins in my fat hands. I jumped over our red stoep, freshly polished the day before by my sister while I'd cut the lawn with garden shears.

As I was leaving, my mother shouted to me: 'And don't take that shortcut of yours you like to take!'

But of course, I promptly disobeyed her and took that Shortcut Of Mine I Liked To Take. Not taking it would have added ten more minutes to my run. I ran everywhere in those days because my grandfather insisted a boy should always be running, especially when sent somewhere by an adult. This habit had stuck with me from the countless errands I'd run during my ten years of living with him, even though I'd now lived apart from him for a few years.

I was wearing dull green military-style cargo pants with multiple pockets, and my brand-new black-and-white Adidas slip-ons, which I loved because of the hundreds of rubber nodes that massaged my feet as I walked.

My shortcut went through Dr Rubusana Training College, which had grounds large enough for a soccer field and a basketball court. The college was named after Walter Rubusana – one of the founders of the South African Native National Congress (SANNC), which later became the African National Congress (ANC).

The fence had a convenient gap in it, possibly created by a fellow shortcut-taker. Once through the college grounds, I jogged across the overgrown veld that was used as a makeshift rugby practice field. It was not an actual field but a patch of hard ground, not at all like the well-kept fields at Hudson Park – the privileged school I now attended. It was also where people often walked home from work. The rugby players and workers going home somehow coexisted in this space. People would be walking from Highway, carrying their bags filled with groceries, and avoiding a fast and furious rugby match at the same time.

I was running along one of the paths created by numerous shortcutters like myself when I noticed a man walking towards me. Just as I passed him, he grabbed my wrist. Before I realised what was going on, the back of my head (inqenstsu) was pressed against his chest, and a cold Okapi knife was at my throat. I froze, steadying my neck.

At that moment, another man came running towards us. I thought he was there to save me. What a foolish young man I was. As soon as he got to us, he gave me two quick authoritative slaps to my soft, freshly Blue Sealed face, and I realised that they were in this criminal enterprise together.

They both wore the universal tsotsi uniform: the hat, the pleated formal pants. Tsotsis also had a distinct sideways-leaning gait, their heads tilted slightly to the right or left, and their arms often clasped behind their backs, with one hand holding the wrist or elbow of the other. This walk was always a telltale sign of danger, but for reasons I can't quite understand, it never occurred to me that I might be in any.

I was asked a question as if I were in an interrogation room, being questioned by the Gestapo: 'Kwedini, iphi le mali?' ('Little boy, where is the money?')

The money was clenched in my hand, two five-rand coins in a tight fist. I did not even have the words to speak at this point, and I unfolded my hand. But they were not pleased.

The second man, the one who had released the slap like a kwaito smash hit, grabbed me by my shirt and said, 'Iphi imali yephepha?' ('Where is the paper money?')

'Andinayo, bhuti!' ('I don't have it, brother!') Though I was crying and begging for my life, I'd even given these hooligans a title of respect – bhuti – that they definitely didn't deserve but which I hoped would help me.

Another slap followed. 'Kwedini, ukuba ndingayifumana imali yephepha apha kwezi pokotho, sakurhuqa siyokubulala kwesa s'kolo and kill you.' ('If we find paper money in these pockets, little boy, we'll drag you to that school over there and end your life.')

I kept repeating, 'Oh yhini Nkosi yam!' ('Oh, Lord, please!'), like an elderly woman. My mind raced to the memory of my father, who had died nearly a decade ago from the wounds of a mysterious knife at the hands of an equally mysterious assailant.

I wasn't sure if there was any paper money in my pockets or not, but I was terrified that there might be, somehow missed when I'd handed my mother's casino winnings back to her the night before. We had been to Amatola Sun Hotel, a casino in Bhisho – my mother had gambled a bit and won some money.

To my eternal relief, they found nothing more. One man kicked me while the other smacked me at the back of my head and barked, 'Voetsek!' As any South African knows, once you hear 'voetsek' you move your feet fast and get the hell out of there.

I fled, running as fast as I could. It wasn't long before I realised I'd left my new slip-ons behind. Glancing back, I saw the two men walking off as if nothing had just happened. One of them was carrying my new shoes.

The incident must have lasted less than a minute, but it felt much longer. Barefoot, humiliated, and angry, I ran home.

When I got back, my mom and sister, Sikelelwa, could see I was in distress. I'd also returned far too quickly to have completed the errand in Highway.

My mother asked, 'Hayibo, kwenzeke ntoni?' ('What happened?')

I was in tears. 'Ndiphakwe inkunzi.' ('I was served a bull [got mugged].')

My mother could never resist saying, 'I told you so.' And told me so, she did.

The profiteering prophetess

My mother's scepticism towards spiritual and traditional healers rubbed off on me early. Occasionally, we'd see a travelling troupe of amagqirha (what Westerners used to refer to as witch doctors but are actually traditional healers). We all held a certain fear and trepidation around amagqirha but my mother used to say, 'Andiwafuni la maxoki.' ('I don't trust these liars.')

As children, whenever we saw a group of travelling traditional healers, we'd run and stay as far from the road as possible. We believed all sorts of myths about them. They were intimidating, and we were gripped by fear because we believed every word of the stories we'd been told. For example, if you upset one, they could turn you into a goat – and by goat, I don't mean Messi.

Amagqirha dressed in cowhide skirts, with leather bangles and black rubber bands on their biceps. Beads of all sizes adorned their wrists, necks, ankles, and sometimes criss-crossed over their chests. Their heads were decorated with a mix of feathers and porcupine quills. To us children, they were a spectacle we found both frightening and fascinating.

Each travelling troupe had drums made from cowhide and enamel, and sometimes we'd hear the rhythmic beat as they walked along the untarred Dutyini village road. They were a rare and electrifying sight. I never understood how they decided whose yard they would stop outside to chant and sing. Thankfully, they never stopped outside ours, and I was grateful for that, as it would have given me a level of anxiety I can barely describe.

My friends and I would follow them from a distance, keeping to the grass at the roadside. When they stopped, we'd quickly lie on our stomachs in the tall grass or peek at them from behind an anthill, thinking we were hidden.

When the amagqirha began stomping and chanting, we'd be transfixed. Their dance was more of a powerful, physical stomp, while holding a cow's tail up, and they would stomp the ground so hard I'd wonder how they were not digging holes or breaking their legs. The rhythmic beat of their feet echoed alongside the drumming, singing, chanting, and clapping.

If one of them happened to leap in our direction during their trance, we'd jump up and scatter – even though we were too far away for them to catch us. Of course, that was if they were even interested in catching us, which they never were. Later, we'd return to our very obvious hiding spots.

The amagqirha weren't the only spiritual group we observed with fascination and fear. There was also a group called the amaZiyoni (Zionists) – various Christian groups without a formal church building. They wore long blue or green tunics with white accents, and their leader was always a man with an unshaved beard and a long staff.

On occasion, we would watch the amaZiyoni from afar as they conducted their service outdoors, seated or standing in a large circle, singing and clapping. Members would take turns spinning in the centre, faster and faster until they fell into a trance. Some would fall onto other members, and the elder would whip them with a sjambok to get rid of the demon that caused the fall. Watching them spin until they were dizzy, only to be beaten for it, left us both horrified and bemused. Being dizzy from spinning seemed like the most normal thing, but here it was treated as something almost otherworldly.

One of my uncles frequently sought the counsel of an umthandazeli (a prophetess and healer), hoping to rid himself of professional and personal misfortunes and achieve financial prosperity. He relied on her to ward off evil spirits and to reverse misfortunes sent his way – the misfortune that had been wished upon his life would be boomeranged back to the sender. One day, he took my sister and me to visit this umthandazeli, a journey that took us to a village not far from Kokstad, driving from Mount Ayliff.

We got off the taxi and walked up a steep hill, passing a number of houses. Along the way, we saw many sickly people, though most of them appeared perfectly healthy; they, too, were hoping that she would turn their fortunes around. By the time we reached her homestead, there were already hundreds of people, mostly women, waiting outside in the heat, some seated on straw mats with umbrellas and food, prepared for the long wait. They had all come here to fetch hope.

The mthandazeli's homestead consisted of a number of stand-alone houses and it seemed that there was an entire economic ecosystem that had blossomed in and around it. Several people had been waiting since the day before and had found lodgings in neighbouring houses and within the homestead. The prophetess's family also ran a shop within the homestead selling items she said were necessary for healing – candles, chickens, and ropes in different colours for protection – all at a premium. She even sold run-of-the-mill white candles that could be found in any home – except that she had supposedly prayed over these, so they demanded a higher price. Conveniently, or miraculously, all these items that were necessary for healing or good fortune had to be bought from her shop at a premium.

I wondered if the candles were even prayed over in the first place. If she did, in fact, pray over them, did she lay her hands on the whole packet to bless them in bulk, or did she do it candle by candle? How did it work exactly? I asked my uncle some of these questions and he assured me that they must be prayed over; otherwise, her miracles wouldn't work. And since people arrived in droves, the miracles must work. I nodded slowly but I felt deeply sceptical. It looked nothing more than some healing cartel to me.

Luckily for us, my uncle had a good relationship with the prophetess, and we didn't have to wait long. We were ushered into a small, dimly lit, rectangular mud-brick room with drawn curtains. She wore a green tunic with layers of white and green underneath, her head wrapped in cloth matching her outfit. A single candle flame danced lazily in the shadows.

She seemed tired and had her elbow on the table, with her head resting on her left hand. As I went to sit down beside her, she immediately recoiled, saying, 'Get away from me,' and gesturing for me to sit as far away from her as possible. She continued to convulse briefly and stopped.

Her reaction left me immediately unsettled. *She definitely sensed evil in me*, I thought, feeling panicked. *What sort of evil am I carrying?* Maybe she knew that I was sceptical.

My uncle introduced us, mentioning that we were the children of his late brother. I hoped that she felt like a jerk now for talking to a fatherless child like that. After a brief conversation, she took an old, battered isiXhosa Bible, one that looked like it had battled through many years of exorcisms and struggles with evil.

She handed a box of Lion matches to my uncle, telling him to toss a matchstick each time she opened the Bible. She would chant, open a page, and as a matchstick landed, she would close the Bible, repeating this several times until enough matches were tossed in. She then began opening the Bible and reading the verse each match was pointing to. This was how my uncle's future and fortunes were read.

For my sister's turn, she did the same with the matchsticks and Bible. The prophetess asked leading questions and my sister answered truthfully. I was still panicking because I was clearly the evil one in the room, but I was also devising a plan to test her and her abilities. I would tell little lies, giving just yes or no answers, and if she was really a prophetess, she should be able to tell if I was lying.

When it was my turn, my heart was racing as I tossed my matchsticks between the Bible pages.

'Does your father work in office?' she asked. How can the all-knowing prophetess not know that my father had died? My uncle had just told her that we were his late brother's children. I saw a loophole.

But a yes or no answer here was not going to be enough. I had to let her know that she was wrong.

'No, he died when I was five,' I clarified. I was still wondering if she was feeling guilty for dismissing a fatherless child with those weird convulsions.

'He died at home?'

This woman is scamming us, I thought.

'No, he died in Johannesburg.'

'But at *home*,' she said, as if to intimidate me into saying yes.

'No, he was stabbed on a bus,' I said. *Heke, I am getting you back.*

She made a few other assumptions that were so off base I lost all faith in propheteering, which really seemed more and more like profiteering off people's despair and desperation. *How does my uncle not see through this?* I wondered.

Even to this day, when I drive down the beautiful winding road from Mount Ayliff towards Kokstad, and pass Zinkawini village where the prophetess used to live, I shake my head, thinking of the people who clung to her promises. Perhaps I understand little of the ways of propheteering, but I do know that the longing to make sense of the unfathomable is deeply human, especially when surrounded by life's seemingly insurmountable challenges. Sometimes, the hope for divine intervention to lift you out of despair can feel like the only possible answer.

My sweet and tragic one-sided romantic affair

When I was in Standard 6 at Hudson Park High School, I was selected to be part of a programme called Tech Prep. I have no idea how the selections were made, but they chose children from Mdantsane, and somehow, I was part of that group. By some remarkable coincidence, my sister was chosen too, as well as Athi Geleba, who is now the head of digital communications in The Presidency. The three of us were Hudsonians.

The programme brought together children from different schools around East London and we met in a building in town. The goal was to prepare us for the wondrous world of technology. To this day, I am not sure what exactly we were meant to learn because we already had computers at school. I don't recall learning anything I didn't already know. But I was glad to leave school during break and be part of this programme.

Little did I know that, at this programme, I would encounter the most beautiful schoolgirl I had ever seen in my life. Her beauty was a fantastic assault to the senses.

My crush was instant. It was the kind of crush that leaves

your mouth as dry as the Kalahari. It was swift and sudden and embarrassing. I was unarmed, and too unprepared to fake nonchalance, so I did my best to avoid looking in her direction.

I could not muster the audacity even to attempt to speak to this goddess. She'd clearly descended from Mount Kilimanjaro to grace this mere mortal from Dutyini now living in Mdantsane with her beauty. I decided that I would admire her beauty from a distance. I didn't want her to know how I felt – that would be so uncool. I mean, I was uncool already but I didn't want to add more uncool factor.

The goddess was from a different school – Alphandale. It was a so-called coloured school in a coloured neighbourhood in East London. Coloured and Indian schools had integrated black pupils into their schools years before white schools.

Thank God, I didn't see her every day because I don't think I could have paid attention to the programme. I only saw her on Fridays, so Friday quickly became my favourite day of the week, because I'd get to not talk to her. Again.

One day, our instructor announced that we were going to work on computers – those old cream-coloured desktops with massive backsides. There weren't enough so we had to share them.

By some miracle, the goddess was paired with me. I goddamn nearly died. This meant that I actually had to talk to her now and not just admire her from a distance (it all seems mildly stalkerish now). I did not need this.

I knew how to use computers because my school had a few. I frequently used the old Apple computer in the school library, where I spent hours making pictures on some program I stumbled upon by accident. I'd even draw Michael Jackson's face, having to be very delicate with the cursor as I 'painted' him. The other kids would stop and ooh and ahh at my creations, which I made sure to show off, hoping maybe one of the attractive girls in the library would talk to me. Sometimes, it worked.

Now here I was with the most attractive girl I'd ever cast my eyes upon. She sat down next to me. Unlike me, she didn't know anything about computers because her school didn't have any, yet there was a sense of self-assurance about her that I found both intimidating and attractive. We sat side by side and she asked me questions as we worked. I gave brief answers without looking away from the screen, determined to keep up a cool, indifferent demeanour.

My fingers were dancing on the keyboard. Miraculously, my hands weren't shaking. Out of the corner of my eye, I could see the red skirt of her school uniform ending halfway down her thighs. The proximity was very exciting for a teenage boy.

Then, out of nowhere, her knee touched mine. My heart raced as if I'd just finished a sprint, and I quickly devised a plan to have our knees divorce without making it obvious. Craftily, I stood up and leaned forward to point at something on the screen. Then, when I sat my ample Xhosa man buttocks back on the chair, I subtly shifted it so that our knees weren't touching anymore. That had been both the greatest and scariest moment of my teenage life.

But then she moved her chair, and our knees touched again! To me, this was the teenage equivalent of having sex.

Years later, we both ended up in Cape Town for our tertiary education, and I saw her once by chance. Though I had grown braver by then, she still evoked the same terror in me. We chatted briefly, and she was just as breathtaking and gloriously beautiful as I remembered.

Life is like that sometimes

One night, I dreamed I ran into her at the train station, under the bridge. In the dream, she gave me her phone number, scribbling it on the palm of my hand, but I accidentally smudged it. When I woke up, I could have slapped myself. I told myself I'd find a way to get in touch with her.

But a few months later, I heard the most tragic news. She'd gone back home to Mdantsane and was taking a taxi when a stray bullet, meant for the driver in a territorial war, struck her. She passed away.

In the end, she remains, in my memory, a perfect snapshot of youthful infatuation and the fragility of life. Her story, brief but unforgettable, is a reminder of how fleeting beauty, innocence and life can be.

The art class model

Once I got to Standard 8 at Hudson Park High School, our practical art lessons were no longer held at the school but at Belgravia Art Centre. Every Thursday, just before the last two periods, the Standard 8s, 9s and Matrics would get on the school bus for the ten-minute drive. Belgravia Art Centre served various schools around East London, so as our bus arrived, another bus from a different school would be departing.

Occasionally, our art teacher would get his helper to sit as our model during lessons. She'd sit on a chair, wearing her domestic worker's uniform and looking utterly uninterested, and we'd paint or draw her. But one day, she walked into class topless, wearing only her panties. There was no warning. We looked into each other's wide eyes, not knowing what the hell we were witnessing. She sat on a chair at the centre of the room, facing us.

A silence, uncommon among the art students, descended like a feather gliding to land on a desk. For 30 seconds, I don't know if any of us drew a breath.

We were used to studying nude paintings, but this was different. The teacher instructed us to get our paintbrushes and begin. We picked up our brushes hesitantly. Conversations that usually filled the room during lessons were replaced by a heavy quiet – at least for the first ten minutes. We were shocked and bemused.

Her face told a story of a hard life. It appeared several decades older than her body, with the lines of an old woman. She must have been in her late thirties or early forties but her face might as well have been 70. The emotional damage and distress that she must have lived with all her life was visible, and her face looked like she might have had a long relationship with alcohol too.

Over time, we got used to it, as people do when exposed to something repeatedly. It's a sobering truth about humanity. We can normalise just about anything, even the things we shouldn't. What had once left us wide-eyed and stunned became just another Thursday at Belgravia, as though this situation had blended into the wallpaper of our lives.

But though painting her became a routine part of our lessons, I could tell that my classmates still felt uncomfortable. I could tell that she didn't want to be sitting there near-naked, being stared at by high school kids. Painting her was always hard for me but, like everyone else, I had marks to get. My own levels of discomfort were certainly more layered. She was a coloured lady, and there were only three people of colour in the class: her, my friend and myself.

Her relationship with her employer, our teacher, who was also the principal of Belgravia Art Centre, was odd. They bickered constantly. I'd never seen any domestic worker argue with their employer like that. After one of their spats, she'd sit in silence for the rest of the class. I often wondered if there was more to their relationship than just employer and employee.

Their dynamic reminded me of the artists he'd teach us about: so many of them seemed to have massive sexual appetites and questionable relationships with their muses, models, or the so-called exotic locals they exploited in distant lands.

The idea of protesting never entered my mind. I doubt it occurred to anyone else either. After all, weren't nude models a normal part of an artist's education, to understand the human body? To us, this was part of the process. Yet, there was an unspoken unease among us. We knew something was off, but we went along with it anyway. Each of us must have found a way to justify it in our minds.

Maybe this is how we let things go in the world – we tell ourselves small justifications until it's too late.

Leaving home and living with my uncle

One of us had to go. And that was me. After I turned sixteen, my mother found it harder to look after four children as a single, unemployed parent. She had kicked her long-term boyfriend, Tununu, out the year before, and while his departure was necessary, it left a financial void that made things even harder. As a single, unemployed parent, she had to make tough decisions, and I was part of the solution.

In the rural Eastern Cape, it was common for your children to stay with extended family. If a certain family member struggled to make ends meet with all their children, another relative would take one or more children in. In English, this is known as a 'ward'. I am not sure if there is an isiXhosa word for it, but it was seen as ukuboleka umntwana (to lend a child) to family. It was not adoption; it was a temporary support system, a cultural safety net that ensured children were cared for within the family.

Taking in a ward was not only for struggling families. Sometimes parents who worked far from home would ask family members to care for their children; for example, if the mother was employed as stay-in help for white people in a distant town or city. Often, the employed parents would thank the extended family member by gifting them a sheep once a year.

Without much discussion, my mother told me that I was to live with my uncle, Vusumzi Mgugudo in NU 16 in Mdantsane. She reminded me that my uncle had a son my age. And that was that. I did not question her decision.

Though I had met Uncle Vusumzi several times when he visited us in NU 3, I couldn't shake a sense of apprehension. Would I get along with his kids? Would I be welcome? Would I feel like an intruder in their home? Of course, I was no stranger to moving around, but I was a bit older now, and had just begun to settle into living with my mother and siblings, a family unit I hadn't truly experienced before. We had spent so little time together as a proper family that we were still figuring out who we were to each other.

In Dutyini, my mother had left when I was three, and I lived with my grandparents and little sister. Then came boarding school, followed by a brief three-year stint living with everyone as a family. Just as I was adjusting to that dynamic, I moved to live with Uncle Vusumzi. My later childhood years resembled a nomadic existence, a constant shifting of homes and relationships, where belonging felt less like a solid foundation and more like sitting on the hard benches at Home Affairs, shuffling up one spot at a time until it was finally your turn to talk to an official.

Uncle Vusumzi's home was a typical township four-roomed house. But there was electricity, a TV and a fridge – all things we did not have. When I had lived at NU 3 with my mother, I used to go to our elderly neighbour, Joyce, to watch the news. Every week, just before the news ended and I was about to go home, she'd heave her large body up off the sofa and walk to her bedroom. A few minutes later, she would shuffle out of the room holding a framed photo. It was a black-and-white photo of her wearing a beauty-queen sash that read: *Miss Rose*.

'Ndandiligqiyazana, intombi entle ngeemini zam.' ('I was a great beauty in my day.') 'You know, I was the most beautiful girl in the whole region, and everyone knew it.'

I'd always offer a surprised and delighted reaction, as if I was hearing this or seeing the photo for the first time, admiring it and saying, 'Wow!' or 'Yho!' or something of the sort. I felt the need to be kind. And besides, I needed to be back here tomorrow night to watch her TV again. If this was the price I had to pay, it was worth it helping an old lady relive her glory days.

Sometimes, when her children were visiting, I could smell the meat boiling in the kitchen, I would hope they would not want to start dishing up while I was still watching the news. I would often excuse myself, and on evenings when they did offer me a plate, I politely declined, as my mother always served supper early and I was already full.

Living at my uncle's house was different. Now, I didn't just watch the news – I could watch whatever was on TV, at any time. It was going to be great. Now, I would be able to participate in conversations about TV shows with the other kids at school. And even better, my uncle's place was one of the first few houses in Mdanstane with a DStv satellite dish. It was such a unique feature on the side of the four-roomed structure that his house was used as a landmark. It was called, 'la ndlu ine satellite' ('that house with a satellite dish').

When I met my uncle's son, Mncedi, I noticed that he was talk, dark and a bit chubby. He had an imposing presence and did not smile. We looked at each with curiosity and a hint of suspicion. But I soon realised that this boy was playful and friendly. He had two younger brothers, Sphendu and Luyolo. We would practise the wrestling we saw on TV on them. A number of plank beds were broken during the two years I stayed at my uncle's.

On Fridays after school, I would sometimes go back to visit my mother and bring my four-year-old brother, Nganga, to stay with me at my uncle's over the weekend. I would take care of him, and he was always happy to hang out.

Along with our other cousins in the house, he enjoyed watching WWE wrestling. He always made me laugh because he called The Undertaker's manager 'Paul Pear' instead of Paul Bearer. Even at his age, Nganga was not exempt from being tossed around during our wrestling practice. He found this highly entertaining.

'Bhut'am, bhut'am, ndiphinde!' ('My brother, my brother, do it again!')

While we didn't walk 20 kilometres to school in the snow ...

Going to a previously whites-only school was something many members of the community marvelled at, but it had its challenges. First of all, the schools were far because many black people still lived in townships and had not moved to the white suburbs as yet. At that time, buying or renting a house in previously white suburbs was infinitely more expensive than sending a child to a school there.

In the early days, Tununu, my mother's boyfriend, would drive my sister and me to school and back. When my mother eventually kicked him out of her house, we had to take minibus taxis. This meant waking up even earlier as we had to navigate the often-unreliable schedules and overcrowded vehicles.

In high school, I soon found out that a friend of mine took the train to and from school. He was saving an enormous amount of money because the train cost a tenth of the cost of a taxi. I was sold, but I never told my mother. I continued the practice of taking the train even when I went to live with my uncle. I made a number of friends who also took the train to schools in East London's suburbs or town. We were the first generation of kids who attended white schools after the fall of apartheid.

The apartheid government spent, on average, eight times more on a white child's education than on a black child's. The difference was apparent not only in the physical appearance of the school buildings, but in the quality of education. The black parents who could manage to send their children to white schools did, even if it meant they had to wake up at least two and a half hours before the white children who lived in the suburbs closer to their schools. In fact, there were a few of my friends who had to wake up even earlier than those of us who lived in Mdanstane. They lived in King Williams Town (now Qonce), which was another 30 minutes away.

I had to be at the train station by 5:30 in the morning to catch the train in case my regular one was late, which happened a few times a week. School started at 7:30 and there was still the 30-minute walk from the station to school. By the time I reached school at 7:00, I'd already been up for hours. I'd read the newspaper in the library until the bell rang. But by 11:30, I'd already been up for seven hours, and I was exhausted. As a child, it never occurred to me that being up so long before most of my classmates might have had something to do with it.

Over and above this, there was also compulsory sport, and getting out of it required a doctor's note. After school, there'd be practice or a match, so we didn't just have our heavy school bags full of textbooks to carry – we also had sports bags to lug around.

In some ways, it's remarkable how much we had to handle. We were up at the crack of dawn, commuting long distances, carrying bags that could rival our body weight, and we were still expected to perform in class and on the field.

Meanwhile, the white kids lived a short distance from the

Life is like that sometimes

school gates, strolling in as if they'd just rolled out of bed.

How we managed to keep up, and even pass, is something I never really thought about back then. But now, I can't help but marvel at the resilience we didn't even know we had. We just got on with it, like it was normal, when really, it was anything but.

My suicide teacher

My biology teacher was a red-haired man with a slow, monotonous voice. He was an authoritarian who would sometimes go off script during his lessons to tell us about his days in the army. Some of his old war stories were even more interesting than the way he taught biology.

His appearance made him seem as strict as he was: he was mostly bald, with patches of hair, which made him look like the former apartheid President FW de Klerk. We black students often suspected he was a bit racist, though he never gave us any solid proof. That's the thing about racism, its plausible deniability. It often exists in the shade of reasonable doubt.

One day, during a nationwide strike by Pick n Pay employees, he gave us a telling moment. Pick n Pay, one of the biggest stores at Vincent Park near our school, was running a go-slow. During the break between classes, a few of us were walking in a group.

'This is not a go-slow, walk fast!' he barked as he passed us.

Our jaws dropped as we looked at each other, wondering if he'd have said that to a group of white students on that particular day.

Another time, he reprimanded a black student for wearing his hair with a deep side parting, resembling a young Nelson Mandela. Later, in biology class, that same student whispered to me, 'He's such a hypocrite – he has the biggest line on his head.' I ugly-laughed, and the teacher asked me if I wanted to share what I was laughing at with the rest of the class. I apologised and assured him that I did not.

The biology teacher also wasn't known for subtlety. At school assemblies, he would scold the whole student body for making noise in the school hall. All the teachers sat facing us on an elevated stage. The principal was closest to the podium, with the deputy beside him. The biology teacher would leave his seat and walk to the podium to threaten us with detention, meaning we'd miss our break and not eat. Of course we'd shut up immediately. He had one catchphrase he used all the time.

'If you act like pigs, I'll treat you like pigs,' he'd say in his Afrikaans accent.

Then one day, when we were making a noise, he got up from his chair and made his way to the podium. I don't know what happened that day or what was in the air, but as soon as he opened his mouth, the whole school shouted, 'IF YOU ACT LIKE PIGS, I'LL TREAT YOU LIKE PIGS!'

The entire hall laughed, including the teachers. At least he had a sense of humour about it – but he still reminded us that he could detain us during break, and the laughter died down quickly.

Our biology teacher brought the same cold authority to his lessons. At least once a term, entire lessons were dedicated to the topic of how to commit suicide successfully. Yes, *successfully*.

It was morbid and disconcerting. Suicide was something I had never heard of anyone in my community doing. It was a 'white people' thing I used to hear about or see on television.

I remember being uncomfortable, shifting in my seat and thinking, *Is this even allowed?* But no one dared to ask him why we were learning this, and he never offered an explanation. I used to listen with horrid fascination, like you'd look at a lion devouring its prey.

He'd go into excruciating detail about what methods wouldn't work, methods that might leave you brain-damaged instead of dead. He explained why carbon monoxide poisoning in a car was a terrible idea, the risks of hanging yourself incorrectly, and even how to cut yourself 'properly' if you wanted to bleed out. He talked about guns too, instructing where to place the barrel for an instantly fatal shot. The sheer clinical nature of his descriptions made it all the more disturbing.

I remember the sense of relief when the bell rang, as if I could exhale for the first time in an hour.

My sister Siki also had him as a teacher. Years later, he'd teach my younger sister, Siku, and my brother, Nganga – Nganga, who would go on to take his own life years later. Of course, I'm not saying this teacher was responsible for what happened, but I can't help but think about it.

I wonder if this teacher believed he was doing some kind of public service, arming us with knowledge to prevent failures if someone was already on the brink. Or maybe it was his way of normalising conversations around something taboo. Whatever his reasons, it felt grotesque at the time, and even now, the memory of those lessons leaves me unsettled.

I think about Nganga and how little we talked about mental

health growing up. In our community, grief and pain were often swallowed whole. Suicide wasn't just not spoken about – it was unimaginable ... until it wasn't.

Swift and sudden transformation to ugly

I discovered early that taking the train instead of taxis saved me an enormous amount of money, even though it added an hour to my walk each day. The train cost only a tenth of my weekly transport allowance, so I soon shared this information with friends who also wanted extra cash without asking their parents for more. All they had to do was avoid mentioning that they now took a cheaper transport option.

After school, I walked to the train station with my usual crew. Once on board, we'd see other kids from various schools in East London, all heading back to Mdantsane. Trains were fairly empty around 3 pm because most people were still at work.

In fact, the trains were only unbearably full with people in the mornings. I'd mastered the art of running alongside the train, grabbing the steel pole, and jumping in while it was moving – or jumping out before it came to a stop. I don't recall ever seeing a girl attempting these tricks. There were a few falls, but I never fell because I wouldn't do any of this if I thought the train was going too fast.

On this afternoon, the train was at about 40% capacity after it picked us up at Vincent station. I rarely sat down – I preferred to stand and chat to friends or walk from carriage to carriage hoping to see familiar or new faces. In fact, I had met a crush on the train. I'd often leave my school bag with a friend and roam around the train for the sake of it.

In one carriage, there was a group of rowdy boys from a school called Commercial Park. It was a private school but it seemed to fall short of the standards of a typical private school or even the so-called Model C schools like my own, Hudson Park.

The group of boys – about a year or two older than me – walked up and down the carriages with a sense of unearned entitlement, dressed in their school uniforms and chequered poor-boy hats – a sign that they had recently graduated from circumcision school and were now men. No longer boys.

But I knew that a recent initiate into manhood is told that he is to act with a sense of decorum and restraint. He is not to be rowdy or arrogant. He should not think he deserves respect; rather, respect is earned. From my observation, these Commercial Park students did not care about the lessons they had been taught.

As the train took off from a station on its way towards Mdantsane, it jerked suddenly, destabilising the passengers' feet and throwing us off balance. I bumped into one of the initiates and he gave me a look, acting like I had just intentionally disrespected him. I brought my hands up, palms open, as a gesture of apology.

In response, he said, 'Owu, ndimdaka mna. Uyandiphatha uphakamise izandla.' ('Oh, so I am dirty, you touch me and then you must raise your hands.')

'Hayi, ibiyitreyini.' ('No, it was the train.')

'Uyandidelela kwedini?' ('You think disrespecting me is okay?')

'Hayi, ndithe uxolo.' ('No, I said I was sorry.')

I didn't want the situation to escalate any further, especially as I could tell that he had been drinking. His gang of men-boys surrounded me with violence hanging in the air like a thin twig, ready to snap at the slightest pressure.

My face was greeted by a humiliating slap – in front of the other passengers, who had decided that they were not going to intervene. Furious, I was about to lunge at him, when he opened his blazer, revealing the biggest knife I had ever seen.

I froze. I was happy to be slapped as many times as they wanted if it meant avoiding that knife. His fist came flying, and I ducked as his gang surrounded me, beating me with a flurry of punches. I hunched over, shielding my head. Not one person said anything, except for one of my schoolmates who called out for them to stop, but when they asked if he'd like a beating too, he was silent. Finally, they backed off, telling me I'd better remember that they are men and I must respect them.

Bruised and humiliated, I stood by myself as the train continued and slowly people came over to me to say they were sorry.

'It's fine,' I muttered.

When the train finally stopped, I disembarked and caught a minibus taxi to NU 16. As I stepped off the minibus, I was about to close the sliding door when it dislodged at the top. *Good God, not another humiliation, I didn't need this now.* The taxi driver turned to glare at me. I quickly put it back in place, but two older women nearby said loudly enough for me to hear, ('Bendingamazi ukuba mbi kangaka lomntwana.' ('I had no idea this child was this ugly.')

I sort of laughed to myself because I suddenly realised why they would say that. I felt the swelling on my face.

When I got home, my cousins were shocked.

I explained what had happened, and they got me ice for my face. In the bathroom mirror, I saw what those women at the station had seen – my face was swollen with bruises and bumps, my lip and eye puffy.

As I put ice on my lips and over the swelling eye, I said to myself, 'Ndimbi nyhani.' ('Turns out they were not lying.')

The next day, I was supposed to go to school but I refused. My new ugly face would be getting stares and I'd have to explain to everyone what had happened. My uncle gave me permission to stay home and I called the school. The principal, Mr Friend, called me back a few hours later. He wanted to know how I'd been beaten up.

I snitched without hesitation. 'I was on the train when it jerked. The leader of the pack slapped me. When I tried to retaliate, he exposed a giant knife in his blazer.'

'What? He had a dagger in his blazer?' the principal asked.

'Yes, sir. A really big one. And then the rest of them all ganged up on me and punched relentlessly,' I said, my anger returning. Even though I knew I hadn't stood a chance against a knife and four bullies, I hated that I hadn't landed a single punch in retaliation. But now it was time to let the snitching do the Lord's work.

'Who else was there?'

I listed my schoolmates who'd witnessed it and would corroborate the story.

Mr Friend's anger grew the longer we spoke. He demanded the names of the culprits, and I sang in the manner of the mob movies, like a canary. I knew at least two names, and the leader of the pack.

He told me he would call their school principal. I was surprised – I had always thought he had a blasé attitude towards his black students. If anything, I thought I was going to be in trouble for missing school. Instead, he seemed determined to seek justice for me.

I could not go to school for a few days. When I eventually returned, Mr Friend took one look at my still-bruised face and, visibly angry, reached for the phone and called their principal again.

I got on the train as usual but didn't see the boys for another week. Their schoolmates told me that the incident had become a scandal at Commercial Park. Their principal told the entire school about the phone call from Mr Friend about certain students' behaviour, and that they'd also been wielding daggers. The students had been suspended and the school was considering whether or not to expel them.

When I ran into them a week later, they were all sheepish. The bravado and machismo had vanished – not only had they surely received beatings at home, but they also seemed aware that their fate with the school somehow depended on me. They were ultra-friendly. Even my jokes were suddenly the funniest jokes they had ever heard. They laughed longer and harder than anyone else. If I had told them to jump, they'd have asked how high, then jumped twice as high just to stay in my good graces.

The pride of being men who had gone to the bush – a status that demanded respect from those who hadn't yet gone through the ritual of traditional circumcision – was gone.

My eighteenth birthday

My Uncle Vusumzi was a relatively tall, dark-skinned man whose demeanour commanded respect without demanding it. In Xhosa, it's called isidima, a dignified presence. He never moved hurriedly, but never walked slowly either. It seemed that if the world were ending, it would wait for him to finish what he was doing.

My cousin, Mncedi, and I called him DC (Disciplinary Committee) because we were always being disciplined for one thing or another – more so my cousin than me. I knew how to act, living at my rich uncle's house, knowing he was doing us a favour, but Mncedi often pushed the limits. Uncle Vusumzi never called us by name but referred to us as 'kwedini' (boy) and if he was summoning the both of us, 'makwedini'.

It was during the June school holidays that my mother asked me to pack my bags and go to live at my uncle's house. A few days after I'd moved in, I ventured outside the typical township four-roomed house and I noticed a group of girls standing along the stop-nonsense fence, well dressed and chatting. They seemed to be waiting for something or someone. When I mentioned to Mncedi later how weird it was that they were all standing there for so long, he replied, 'They're not going anywhere; you are new meat. Every time you go out the house, they start talking loudly.'

They were all pretty, but there was one standout for me. I would later find out that her name was Thabisa. She stood far enough from the others to catch attention but wasn't too obvious.

Over time, we all became friends. My cousin was very attracted to our neighbour, Asanda, while she seemed to enjoy stringing him along. I only realised that she'd liked me all along when she suddenly kissed me one day on the way to the shop to get bread. She was passionate and prone to expressing anything she was feeling at any given moment.

A year later, my uncle built a prefab, free-standing flat where Mncedi and I would share a room. One day, before it was complete, Asanda came to visit. We were chatting and joking around near the gate when suddenly, she walked towards me, opened the door of the almost-complete flat, pushed me inside, closed the door behind us and began to unzip my pants.

I immediately panicked. She seemed to be on a mission. My cousins were outside. I zipped my pants back up and opened the door.

As I emerged from the prefab, I kept repeating, 'Wenza ntoni, Asanda?' ('What are you doing, Asanda?')

She ran out of the gate, saying, 'Bendifun' ukubona ukuba uzakwenza ntoni!' ('I wanted to see what you'd do!') I don't know if she was embarrassed or insulted because she then said, 'Uyigay!' ('You're gay!')

'Ngenxa yuba ndingafuni undikhulule?' ('Just because I won't let you unzip my pants?')

She didn't talk to me for weeks after that, making sure I knew

I'd annoyed her. She visited our house much more frequently than she ever did but would walk right past me as if I were invisible.

Asanda was lively and passionate, while Thabisa was reserved and guarded, with long, straightened hair tied into a neat bun. In my eyes, Thabisa was the most beautiful girl in the neighbourhood. She was rumoured to be dating the son of a very prominent boxing trainer who had produced a few world champions from Mdantsane.

We barely exchanged a few words each time we saw each other, and conversations were only ever in a group, where we were all talking to each other. The two of us behaved this way towards one another for nearly two years, even though I liked her. I just could not bring myself to tell her.

On my eighteenth birthday, my uncle gave me and Mncedi money to throw a small party, as our birthdays were only days apart. We bought cake and JC Le Roux and some other refreshments. My other female cousins had cooked a great lunch.

Mncedi and I were seated at a tiny table in front of our guests, who were mostly other cousins and our friends from the area. Some of them included Asanda's male cousins – we were very good friends with them.

Unbeknownst to me, they had decided to make Thabisa our 'Miss Party', and as soon as she walked in, she was made to plonk herself next to me on the bench. Now I was sandwiched between Mncedi and Thabisa in front of the cake, feeling both pleased and embarrassed.

She was also clearly embarrassed. In the photo I have, she's sitting next to me, looking down with a faint smile pressed into her lips. When I look at it now, she reminds me of a shy makoti with her downward gaze.

They clearly put her next to me because they knew we had crushes on each other, but neither of us did anything about it – even after that day. I was terribly shy and I avoided her for weeks afterwards.

She had to walk past our house to reach the shops, and I made sure to stay indoors whenever I saw her passing. My mischievous cousins would rush out, trying to drag me with them. As she walked past, they'd shout, 'Khaya says hi! Do you want him to walk you to the shops?' Thabisa would walk past without saying anything.

Aaah, the folly of youth.

The pots that ended my celibacy

The life of a bachelor is often simple when it comes to possessions, and mine has been no different, especially when I was younger. Being celibate and so unencumbered by material things, I could have been mistaken for a monk in my early twenties – except, of course, for the thick dreadlocks on my head. All my worldly goods could fit into a VW Golf – everything, apart from the single bed I owned.

I lived in Pinelands, Cape Town, for seven years, and during that time, I was celibate, so my single bed remained pure. The suburb was quiet, and in the early 2000s, I was often the only black person in that part of Pinelands. I did my grocery shopping at the Spar, rented movies from Mr Video, and ordered ribs from Steers. The cashiers at the shopping centre were friendly and would always try to strike up conversation with me. I would talk to them but made sure not to become overly familiar. I was wary of any forces that could disturb my celibacy.

Aside from the bed, I didn't own much – no pots, no plates, not even a spoon. When I moved out of the digs, my housemates gave me mismatched cups, plates, and utensils. It was the first time I felt somewhat grown-up.

After moving to Plumstead, I was still happy with my single plank bed – until I started dating a beautiful young woman from Johannesburg. She and I had met at the Loeries advertising awards, where she bumped into me at an after-party. Only later did she reveal, 'Did you think I was bumping you for my health?' That bump led to dating, and eventually, plans for her to visit me in Cape Town.

That's when I realised my single plank bed with its flimsy sponge mattress wouldn't be sufficient. She might think less of me. I was panic-stricken. It so happened that my little brother, Nganga, was also going to be with me at the same time. He was still in school and often came to stay with me during school holidays all the way from Mdantsane in the Eastern Cape.

I had been celibate (voluntarily I might add) for some eight to nine years and never worried about having to share a bed with someone. But now it was time for an upgrade.

On a Saturday morning, a few days before my new girlfriend's arrival, I sprung (excuse the pun) into action, looking for a furniture store. I asked my brother to come with me to Claremont to get a double bed, duvet and sheets.

Wandering down a busy main road in Claremont, we passed a Lewis furniture store. There were some beds on sale, which appealed to me. We walked in and looked at various beds. The salesperson told me about all of them and why one was better than the other. At some point, he started telling me about a bed with extra thick and comfortable layers, blah, blah, blah. All I wanted was a double bed. Then he said, 'And it comes with a set of free pots, the ones you see over there.'

This was a scam I was prepared to die for – or live for. I didn't really care about the extra-thick mattress layer; I just

Life is like that sometimes

wanted those pots. Up until that moment, getting fancy pots hadn't even occurred to me. I had thin, enamel cookware. But with these expensive-looking, thick-based pots, I figured I might appear responsible, even grown-up.

The bed and complimentary pots arrived just before her visit, and it was perfect timing. My self-imposed celibacy came to a sudden halt.

I still use those pots today, plus two more I've added over the years. I doubt I would have owned any for a long time if it hadn't been for that first double bed I bought many years ago.

I suppose the store's promotion made sense after all. Everybody needs to eat and sleep. Sometimes with someone else. And not necessarily in that order.

When I lost my voice (literally)

At the beginning of 2014, I was without my voice for two months. For some people, this was a pleasant, peaceful period.

For a couple of years before that, I lost my voice intermittently and sometimes had a hoarse voice. As a self-diagnoser, I was convinced that these symptoms were the result of secondhand smoke – as a non-smoker, my vocal cords were ultra-sensitive.

Then one Monday, during a sushi dinner with friends, Trevor Noah told me that he suspected I suffered from the same affliction as he did. A few months before, he had been forced to cancel big comedy performances because he had lost his voice in the middle of his stand-up show. He couldn't get a word out. An ear, nose and throat specialist (ENT) discovered a growth, barely the size of a pinpoint, on his vocal cords, and he had surgery to remove it.

I told him no way: not only am I not a professional performer but I was convinced that my self-diagnosed allergy to secondhand smoke was to blame.

'There is no harm in you going to see my doctor to check it out,' he said, giving me his doctor's details.

A few weeks went by and after yet another hoarse-voiced Sushi Monday with friends, Trevor asked if I had made an appointment.

'I haven't,' I admitted.

'Why not? I really think you have it, Khaya,' he said.

'Okay, okay, fine. I will,' I committed.

But later that week, I still hadn't made an appointment. I was at work when I received a text from Trevor: 'Yo, K, I've made an appointment for you.' He gave me a time and date.

I now had no choice but to go.

Fortunately for me, the doctor was no more than a 50-metre walk from Coca-Cola, my place of work at the time, so on the day of the appointment, I walked across the street. When I got to the doctor's office, I found Trevor having his final check-up. He'd deliberately scheduled his follow-up before my appointment to check that I showed up. He got a clean bill of vocal cord health from the man who would now become our doctor.

After Trevor left, I was asked to sit in what looked like a dentist's chair.

The doctor began explaining what he needed to do.

'I am going to put this camera down your nostril,' he said, as if that was the most normal thing to say.

'Down my what?' I asked.

He pulled out a terrifying, snake-like object. After managing to convince me that this contraption would not cause my death, the uncomfortable invasion began. I felt the metal go into my nostril and down the back of my throat. The back of my tongue began the futile exercise of pushing it out. My breathing was laboured, and I was asked to make several sounds.

I was so relieved when he was done.

The doctor vanished into another room for a few minutes, but when he returned, he said, 'I am sorry – I have to go through the other nostril.' I had no choice but to agree.

After the repeated ordeal, he disappeared again, eventually emerging with high-definition printed images of what appeared to be an ugly vagina but was actually my vocal cord area.

He waved the vagina in front of me and said, 'You have polyps growing on your vocal cords. I have been doing this for a very long time, but these are the biggest I have ever seen. Don't be alarmed but when I first saw them, I thought it was cancer, which is why I had to go through your other nostril the second time. I am happy to say that it's not cancer.'

My mind was still processing what he was saying.

'The good thing is we can operate and remove them,' he said.

I was told by the specialist that if I didn't have the giant polyps removed, I was in real danger of never speaking again. Your vocal cords have no pain receptors, so when there is something wrong, it's hard to know.

As it turns out, Dr Trevor Noah was right. I sent him a picture. 'You know how the internet will show you the worst of something or the biggest?' he said. 'I've never even seen one as big as yours on the internet.' Trevor knows his stuff.

I was not allowed to speak for three weeks before and after the operation. My cousin Xolisa Dyeshana likes to call this period the time when he won a lot of arguments against me.

On the day of the operation, I arrived at the hospital early and was shown to my room. I was told I would have to take my clothes off and wear the hospital's finest fashion wear.

One of my garments was a gown that covered my front but exposed my rear end. The nurse also handed me something else, which I put on my head. It was made out of a light-blue material that reminded me of those disposable headcovers restaurant staff wear to avoid hair falling into the customers' food.

When I was done, the nurse drew the curtains back. She took one look me and let out the loudest laugh and walked out.

I was confused.

A few seconds later, she appeared with several other nurses. They also laughed, left, and came back with another group to laugh at me.

After doubling down and rolling on the floor, my nurse eventually said, 'No, Mr Dlanga, that's not for your head. That's underwear.'

The accidental makoti

It was December in the mid-2010s, and I was spending it with my then-girlfriend – our first December together. Any self-loving South African knows that December is not just a month – it's a culture. It is a movement. It has a spirit of its own. When other months dream, they dream of being December in South Africa.

As always during the December holidays, I made the pilgrimage from Johannesburg to East London. This time, for the first time, I had my girlfriend with me. Back then, East London was undoubtedly the capital city of December in South Africa. Many of us leave our homes and families in the Eastern Cape for larger cities in search of better opportunities. In December, we assemble in our home province. It was important for me to be there to see my family – and, of course, to pay my respects to the capital city of December.

After the long drive, we didn't do much that first evening except rest. The next morning, I was woken by a phone call from my mother.

'Your uncle Mavela's wife has passed away. We just got news from Thokoza,' she said.

'What?' I sat up, wide awake now.

'She had been ill for some time,' my mother added. 'I need you to drive me and Lulu to Dutyini today to be with the family.' Her sister was Nolulama, whom she called Lulu.

Selfishly, my first thought was how this news would disrupt my holiday. Would I have to stay in the village until the funeral? As if she could read my mind, my mother reassured me, 'You can just drop us off and come back. Lulu and I will represent the family at the funeral.'

I felt relieved, but also guilty for feeling relieved. I might have even pulled a small, controlled fist pump (which only added to my guilt).

I told my girlfriend about the call and began talking through my options. The Eastern Cape is vast, and the journey from Mdantsane to Dutyini takes six hours one way. After the nine-hour drive from Johannesburg the previous day, I wasn't up for twelve hours of driving in one day. Besides, simply dropping my mother and aunt off without staying to show my respects was out of the question. Not only would it be culturally inappropriate, but it just didn't sit well with me, especially considering that I was not going to be at the funeral. I was going to have to spend a day in Dutyini.

I decided that I was not going to leave my girlfriend by herself for that long in a town she did not know. So I told her that it was best that she joined me on the trip with my mother and aunt. We left the B&B we'd booked, and headed to to Mdantsane to pick up my mom and my aunt. My girlfriend didn't say much, but I could tell she was apprehensive about the trip.

When we arrived at my mother's house in Mdantsane, she and my aunt were already waiting outside with their bags. My girlfriend and I got out and I introduced them. My mother surprised me by immediately warming to my girlfriend. My mom could be pretty playful, and out of the blue, she tickled my partner playfully and even tried to pick her up. Everything seemed peachy, right?

With the bags loaded in the car, it was time to sort out the great dilemma: front seat politics! Who was entitled to the front seat now: the girlfriend or the mother?

I watched as my girlfriend hesitated, clearly weighing whether to take the front seat or defer to my mother. I could see the terror in her eyes. I decided to stay out of this delicate political game, not wanting to risk becoming collateral damage. She eventually opened the rear door, and my mother, without missing a beat, said, 'Uyaphi?' ('Where are you going?') and climbed into the back with her sister. I was relieved it had played out like this. I wanted my girlfriend next to me.

The long drive began, and so did the interrogation. From the back seat, my mom and aunt started cross-examining my girlfriend: Where are you from? What do you do? Do you have siblings? What do your parents do? Where are your villages? Why can't you speak Xhosa?

Eventually, they tired themselves out and began chatting about sisterly matters. Occasionally, I reached over to touch my girlfriend's leg, only to remember the two pairs of eyes in the back seat.

Six hours later, we arrived in Dutyini. I had been driving slower than I would have liked because the two women at the back complained about my driving. They were now expert drivers.

When we arrived, we were greeted by the sound of mournful singing. We were then served food. My girlfriend, having finished eating last, placed her plate on the floor with the others. As she was about to sit back down, I was thinking, *I wouldn't do that*, when my mother piped up: 'Hayibo, wahlala phantsi? Are these dishes going to take themselves to the kitchen?'

I knew how awkward this whole thing was for my girlfriend. She was Tswana (well, she still is) and I am Xhosa. In our culture, the youngest person present clears the dishes after a meal. Shame, she felt embarrassed because it was exactly what she had wanted to do but wasn't sure if it was culturally appropriate. Later, she told me how mortified she had felt, as it's precisely what she would have done back home. Though embarrassed, she quickly took the plates to the kitchen.

As the day wound down, the moment of truth came: sleeping arrangements.

Did I not get the shock of my life when they prepared the rondavel for me – and her – to sleep in!

You prepare a rondavel before my enemies, I thought. Khaya 23:5.

My first therapist

The first time I went to see a therapist, it was to understand why I didn't want marriage and children. This wasn't the primary driving factor, though. My girlfriend at the time was concerned that I did not want to have children or get married. While I loved kids and strongly believed in the institution of marriage, I just did not want it for myself. We'd been together for a few years, and we had now come to a crossroads.

I had a very specific condition for choosing a therapist: they had to be black. I felt there were cultural nuances I wouldn't have to explain – things they would simply know – and that was important to me if I was going to start therapy. My friend, Sindi Ndlovu, had mentioned a great therapist and recommended her to me.

I decided to brave it out and make the call. The therapist was based in Centurion, which meant driving from Sandton would be quite the trek, but I made the appointment anyway. I was eager and curious to see how it all worked – beyond the dramatised sessions I'd seen in movies.

On the day of my first session, I drove from the Heineken offices in Sandton to Centurion just before the afternoon rush hour. When I finally arrived, I was greeted by a sign that read 'Vista Psychiatric Clinic'. An overwhelming sense of embarrassment hit me when I saw that word – psychiatric.

Good heavens, I thought. *I hope no one's at reception. They'll think I'm crazy – or secretly wonder what made me crazy enough to come here.*

Almost immediately, I felt ashamed of my embarrassment. Why should I feel this way about seeking help to understand myself better?

At reception, I masked my awkwardness by pretending to be calm and confident. The receptionist pointed me to a labyrinth of passages that offered no comfort. Finally, I found the room – one of the last down the corridor. The door was slightly ajar, but I knocked anyway.

'Come in,' came a voice from inside.

My first instinct was to judge her office. It was minimalistic, with furniture that gave the impression it belonged to a struggling school or perhaps an old apartheid-era government office. Her chair and mine were synthetic plastic, designed to look like wood, with silver steel rods.

This is not what therapy looks like in the movies, I thought. *Where's the soft couch?*

I tried to stay engaged, but I had already decided I wouldn't return the following week. I'd spend my hour, part with my money, and then part ways with her.

She dived into small talk – her day, her children – and I felt like my time was being wasted. *What was Sindi thinking when she recommended this lady to me?* I wondered.

But about ten minutes into this dull conversation, I found myself talking. Really talking. My thoughts spilled out before I even realised what was happening.

My goodness. She's good, I thought. *How did she get me to open up already?*

When our session was done, I got in my car and smiled to myself. I just could not believe how wrong I had been about her, and how quickly she'd dismantled my preconceived notions. *She's brilliant,* I thought. And to think, I had already decided I wasn't coming back. Next week Monday seemed too long to wait to go back again.

There was a professional and respectful motherly quality about her that I did not expect. At first, I assumed she'd lean more into the motherly side and less into professionalism, but I was wrong. She struck a perfect balance.

Now that I had been to therapy, I could no longer understand why I ever felt that it was a sign of mental weakness. I became a strong advocate for it, sharing its benefits with anyone who would listen. If nothing else, I would tell them, it helps you clarify parts of your life you've neglected or falsely believed would magically sort themselves out on their own.

The R2 million gwinya

I had a helper who came to clean my apartment every Thursday. There wasn't much for her to do, really, since I was a bachelor. I don't cook – I either eat out or order in.

One Thursday, I had a work meeting close to home, but it was cancelled just as I was about to arrive. The worst part was that it was already mid-afternoon so going back to the office made no sense. By the time I'd dealt with traffic and placed my bum on my office chair, I'd have to pack up again and head home.

And so, on this particular Thursday, I got home from work earlier than usual. I had my backpack slung over my shoulder and reached into my pocket to grab my key. As I unlocked the door to my apartment, I saw my helper busy in the kitchen. A beautiful aroma hit me as I turned to lock the door behind me. Her head snapped around quickly, as if she'd been caught doing something she shouldn't have been. She stood frozen, staring in my direction.

She was at the stove, wearing her apron with a dishcloth draped over her left shoulder. She did not move.

I could hear the 'hlwi hlwi hlwi' sound of oil popping in a

pot, and the delicious smell filled the air. As I walked past her, I greeted her, noticing dough turning golden brown in a pan. She was frying amagwinya (otherwise known as vetkoeks – and if you're not South African, Google is your friend). There were already a few of them in a large bowl.

She remained frozen as I put my bag down and went to the kitchen to grab something to drink from the fridge.

Eventually, she found her voice and the ability to move. She explained that she was going to a funeral the next day and wanted to bring something for the family, apologising for making amagwinya at my place.

I told her there was no need to apologise. 'You can use the stove whenever you want. Akukhonto.' It was no problem.

I glanced at the ingredients near the stove, and it was then that I noticed she was frying the amagwinya in olive oil. *Nkosi yam.*

Not knowing much about cooking, I always bought the most expensive oil on the shelf, convinced that the price meant it was healthier. Olive oil is expensive as it is.

I figured that she must have assumed olive oil was like any other cooking oil. I smiled through gritted teeth and told her again there was no need to apologise – she could cook whatever she wanted in the kitchen.

It was basically R2 million per gwinya. The priciest in all the land. While I kept up my polite smile, I realise that there was no point in being upset. I'd never explained the difference between olive oil and normal, everyday sunflower oil, so how could she have known. Besides, it made for a very entertaining story for my colleagues on Monday. They all laughed until tears trickled down their faces.

One of the loudest laughers was Linda Apie, who, only a

few weeks later, walked into my office to say, 'You won't believe what happened yesterday. My helper did what yours did – she made amagwinya with olive oil.'

It was my turn to laugh.

VIP seat with a side of humility

Sometimes, I'm invited to prestigious events and even get seated at the VIP table – because, for whatever reason, someone has decided that I'm meant to be important that day.

One such day arrived when I'd get to be important for two hours. Not only had I been invited to be a judge at this prestigious marketing event, but I'd also been asked to deliver a 30-minute keynote speech on the state of the marketing industry and the need for diversity. Clearly, I was going to be at the 'important' table with the 'important' people, though, in reality, every other person in that room was far more important than I was. I was there on some kind of cosmic stretch.

When my name was called, I stood up, walked to the Perspex podium, and launched into an impassioned speech that I hoped would leave the room shaking. The room was more than 90% white, and I couldn't understand why the industry remained so untransformed. So, I addressed the issue head-on, calling for progress and greater inclusivity in the industry.

I fired off facts, figures and statistics, backing every point with conviction, while addressing this audience of industry executives – something I'd never dreamed of doing as a young boy growing up in a rural village. There was a table of black attendees at the back, and I noticed them nodding and exclaiming in agreement. There was even a politician at the event, nodding vigorously. I felt my spirits rise.

There was one downer: my fly. Somewhere between the indignation and the inspiring figures, I was oblivious to the fact that my zip was down. *Gravity: 1. Me: 0.*

There I was, gesturing with all the confidence of a man convinced he was commanding the room, entirely unaware that my zip was failing me. The transparent Perspex podium also meant that everyone could see it. And the worst part? My tie – the ultimate snitch – was pointing directly at the scene of the crime, like a bright-red arrow just begging people to look. You really can't even trust your own clothes.

But that was only one lesson in humility. Life has a great way of reminding us not to take ourselves too seriously and it would not be long before my next public embarrassment.

Fast-forward to 2018, pre-Musk era, when I was invited by Twitter to be part of a panel discussion, along with other marketing and social media experts.

As I plonked my Xhosa ass on the chair, I was introduced and my achievements, or lack thereof, were read out. Whenever my CV is read out to an audience, I'm hit with a wave of embarrassment, followed by imposter syndrome.

During the discussion, I did my best to sound eloquent and intelligent. As a non-native English speaker, I brought my best English with me that day. I even fetched the highbrow English I had on reserve. I featured words such as: *tantamount*, *quantum* (not to be confused with the public transportation vehicle), *defenestrate*, *amalgamate*, and *photosynthesis*. Ndithini na? I even used phrases like 'at this juncture in time'.

There were about 70 people in the audience and every now and then, I would catch people nodding in agreement or smiling. I figured I was doing all right.

While doing my utmost to sound intelligent and impressive, I happened to glance down at my feet. Another strike by my wardrobe. I was wearing mismatched sneakers.

Before the afternoon panel, I had been in the office all day. I'd walked from one meeting to another, talking to people in hallways, pointing and laughing, printing, signing documents, and saying things like, 'approved' and 'no, I can't meet on that day – I have back-to-backs'. Well, during all those interactions, not a single soul told me I was wearing different sneakers. Perhaps they thought it was some fashion-forward statement by Adidas, but I assure you, I am not that trendy.

Noticing this fashion faux pas, all my efforts to appear sophisticated evaporated. In the middle of some important point, I screamed in pure horror: 'Aaaaah! I've been wearing a different sneaker on each foot the whole time?' Laughter filled the room, and with a resigned sigh, I accepted that of all my accomplishments, it was this fashion fail that would be my legacy here.

Kubi emhlabeni kodwa siyaqhuba.

December: Season of chancers

Every South African looks forward to December. The closer it gets, the hungrier and more desperate we get for it.

In fact, it could be argued that December begins in October. The alcohol brands know it because they start throwing parties halfway through October, lubricating us for the fun times to come.

For many, it's a time of joy and celebration. But for others, who do not have the means to participate in the festivities, it can be a stark reminder of how difficult life is.

It's also the season for heists, cash-in-transit robberies, and scams. Some criminal elements are looking for a quick buck so they can spend with abandon. From October through December, I was nervous about driving near cash-in-transit vans because they were robbed at significantly higher rates during this time. At any moment, a heist could go down.

It is also a time for people to take chances. A few years ago, I had driven from East London to Gqeberha with my cousin, Xolisa Dyeshana. Not long before, he had been in a car accident. His car was completely written off, and he survived what could have been a tragic crash with his then-girlfriend. When the paramedics arrived, they told him he was lucky to be alive, as many accidents in that area had no survivors. They credited the type of car he was driving for saving their lives. He broke his ankle and was trapped upside-down in the car for two hours in the rain before being rescued. Two days later, screws drilled into his bones and crutches in hand, he still fulfilled his duties as the best man at our friend Sakhi Madikane's wedding. If you know Xolisa, you'll know that no near-death experience could ever stop him from having the time of his life – and certainly not in December.

After a night of Gqeberha December festivities, I decided to stop by the McDonald's drive-thru on my way to the hotel. It was around 3 am. I pulled up behind a car that had already placed an order. After a minute or so, a woman stepped out of that car and approached my window.

She was absolutely gorgeous. She knocked on my window, and for a moment, I thought, *Oh wow, I'm about to be hit on in a drive-thru for the first time!*

'I've come to ask you to pay for our food,' she said.

This gentleman was too stunned to speak initially. 'Why?' I asked. She did not even greet me before making demands for her and her friends.

'Because I'm asking,' she responded.

'No. I don't know you.'

'So? Surely you can afford it – it's only McDonald's!' she retorted.

'If it's only McDonald's, why can't you pay?' I jabbed back.

She tried another tactic – shame. 'If you can't afford it just say so.'

'I can't afford it,' I said, because I am shameproof to such antics.

Life is like that sometimes

'How can you not afford it when you drive such a fancy car?' she asked, folding her arms and pulling a face of disgust. Even with the ugly expression she wore, she was still insanely gorgeous.

'Because all my money goes into my car. That's why I can't afford it.'

She turned and went back to her car in a huff. The audacity!

The audacious thief

I have a pair of round, black-rimmed Lindberg glasses. Above the bridge, at the apex of each rim, a thin gold bar connects the two rounded sides, tapering down into handles that go just above the ears. Thin, light, and relatively pricey, they're a favourite pair – flexible enough not to break if you accidentally sit on them.

In August 2018, I was visiting my hometown of East London and hired a rental car after landing at the airport – an elegant, state-of-the-art automatic Avanza, because your boy can't drive a manual. When people ask why and judge me for it, I tell them it's like being proud of driving a chariot. Manuals are relics of the past.

While there, I gave people free lifts, unknowingly placing my life at risk since taxi drivers don't take kindly to anyone threatening their business. When I returned this grand vehicle to the airport, I got on my flight wearing my prescription shades. It was only after I landed in Cape Town that I realised I had left my regular glasses behind – most likely in the Avanza or at the hotel.

I called the rental company. A few hours later, I got a call back informing me that they hadn't found any glasses in the vehicle. I figured I must have dropped them somewhere; they were so light I might not have even heard them fall. I decided not to pursue it further.

Later that year, in December, I drove all the way from Cape Town to East London to spend Christmas with my family. I enjoy long drives on my own because I get to think and hear the hum of the engine. There's also something awe-inspiring about driving through the Huguenot Tunnel, knowing that thousands of tons of rock hang above you, held at bay by human ingenuity. I usually avoid the beautiful, winding Garden Route because I prefer the flat, open Karoo roads where you can see for kilometres ahead. Every now and then, I pass a small, forgotten town, with only a handful of people who probably stay because they have nowhere else to go.

While I typically drive to East London, I rarely drive back, choosing instead to ship my car back to Cape Town. At the end of my trip, after dropping my car off at the airport, I decided to try my luck at the rental company to see if I could find my glasses. This time I could show them a photo on my phone to help the search.

The polite staff behind the counter listened to my story and looked at the photo. They opened a cabinet filled with lost and found items. There were several boxes filled with various pairs of glasses and they rummaged through them one by one in front of me. After about ten minutes, they started on the last box.

At that moment, a gentleman emerged from the back to assist another customer. We were separated by a small pillar, but I could still see him clearly – especially because he was wearing black, round glasses that struck a precise resemblance to mine.

My head jerked around in shock, and I craned my neck around the pillar to get a closer look. I glanced back at the staff and mouthed, 'Those are my glasses.'

If their eyes could have popped out of their faces they would have. They froze, unsure whether to feel embarrassed or laugh. Observing their paralysis, I decided to intervene. I apologised to the customer as I interrupted them, and got straight to the point: 'Those are my glasses.'

He remained silent for several heartbeats, likely wondering what to do. It was like catching a criminal who'd got away with his crime for so long that he'd forgotten he'd committed it. I half-expected him to tell me the glasses were his. Lucky for him that he didn't because I would have asked him to take them off to check for my name, which was engraved in tiny letters along the rim, visible only if you looked closely enough.

Finally, he found the words to speak. 'I know, I had them for safekeeping.'

I blinked, thinking, *isibindi esingaka*! The audacity.

His colleagues began busying themselves, wanting to hear the juice but also wanting to hide. Judging by their eyes and pursed lips, they were suppressing both shock and laughter.

He seemed paralysed, just looking at me, not knowing what to say. I felt like we had entered a staring contest and next to us was the poor customer, watching this unexpected drama series.

'Well, can I have them back please?'

He removed the glasses, handing them over. I noticed that the protective rubber grips around the ears were slightly damaged, probably from his 'safekeeping'. I decided not to report him – Christmas was two days away, and it would be stupid to lose a job over a pair of glasses.

When I later posted about the incident on Instagram,

Life is like that sometimes

a user by the name of Phumlani Mayekiso, commented in Xhosa saying, 'Ukuba yile igreen indawo ebolekisa ngemoto, ndazibona ndazincoma. Ndabuza ukuba iyafumaneka iLindberg eMonti, kwathiwa uyiphathelwe eGoli. Enjalo iliver nyhani.' ('If it is the green car rental company, I complimented him about them. I asked if one can find Lindbergs in East London. He said someone brought them from Johannesburg for him. Very cheeky, indeed!')

That guy ... he certainly had enough sbindi for all of us.

From Davos with vengeance

Folks who live in Amsterdam would claim it was a warm, sunny day – but it was far from this South African's idea of a warm day when a DM landed in my Instagram inbox, asking me if I was in Amsterdam. It was from a lady who ranks high on the attractiveness scale. I knew her from back home – more than just knowing. We also knew each other in the biblical sense. It had been some time since we last did the dance of the bodies, but we were both single and had the option to mingle.

She wanted to know how much longer I was going to be in the city. I was there for work but had decided to take a few extra days off to enjoy Amsterdam without worrying about meetings. She was in Davos and told me that she'd be flying over to spend some time with me. I was thrilled. We were about to have a completely unplanned European winter romance, even if just for a few days.

When she arrived, I took her to one of my favourite restaurants. All the tables in the restaurant were downstairs except for one, which you had to reach by climbing a steep wooden staircase. The place had eclectic decor – it was small but probably offering the tastiest, homeliest food in all of

Amsterdam, perfect for those cold days. We enjoyed a delicious meal, sharing giggles and catching up.

Our daytime walk around the city gave the impression of two lovers lost in each other while discovering the city. Her face held a constant, inviting smile that concealed a sharp mind. I was thrilled that she had flown in from Davos entirely of her own volition to see me.

What a man I must be, I thought, walking like someone who had just discovered he was the master of the universe. Even my jokes were quicker and wittier than usual. Having a woman fly in from another country for you can inflate your ego beyond Trumpian levels.

That evening, we had dinner and visited a beautiful bar at the Waldorf where she was staying. Her hotel was significantly more upmarket than mine – if hers was a five-star, mine was a two.

The bar at the Waldorf had been repurposed from an old bank vault, with safety deposit boxes incorporated into the decor. It was dimly lit, with only a handful of patrons. We joked with the two barmen, dressed in white shirts, black waistcoats and bow ties. We ordered whiskies and took shots. Peak flirtation was at play. It was a carefree, almost whimsical day – one of those you'd read about in a romance novel, free from any weighty matters. It was one of those days Hemingway might have written about, where the simplicity of the moment held its own quiet significance.

We flirted between drinks as usual. I leaned in for a kiss on the lips.

'Nothing is going to happen,' she said, a smile still on her face as she moved away from the kiss.

'Really?' I raised my eyebrows, thinking she was clearly

teasing. How could we not pick up where we had left off? After all, we were in Europe.

'No, Khaya, I am serious. You know what you did,' she said, her tone now firm.

'What do you mean? What did I do? What did I do where?' I asked, moving closer to rub her thigh beneath the bar.

'You really don't remember what you did?' she continued, her smile still in place.

'I don't know what I did. I am so confused,' I protested.

'Remember Xolisa's birthday in December?' she asked.

'Of course I remember X's birthday, it was a lot of fun, and you were there too.'

'Do you remember what you did?' She seemed so certain about this supposed crime I had committed, but I knew for a fact that I hadn't done anything deserving of any kind of sanction.

'It was just a bunch of people having a good time,' I said, still baffled.

'Do you remember coming to me, pushing me against a wall, and giving me the most passionate, unprovoked kiss?' she asked.

I remembered the exact moment – where we were and even the person she had been standing with at the time. Panic set in as I wondered if I'd crossed a boundary. While we were both single, we still ... well, vibed. Perhaps when I kissed her, there was someone else she had her eye on, and I unknowingly blocked her. Or had I done something worse?

'I am so sorry if I offended you or if you were with someone else and I jeopardised that. I am really sorry for assuming that you and I were still like that, if that wasn't the case,' I said, feeling horrible. What on earth had I been thinking?

'No, the kiss wasn't a problem at all. It was lovely – absolutely perfect – and it was exactly what I wanted. The best part was I didn't expect it. That's not what I am mad about.'

'Then I am confused. What's this about?' I asked, still trying to piece it together.

'Khaya, you really don't know what you did? You don't kiss a girl like that – the way you did – then just leave her and not take her home with you. You pushed me against the wall, we kissed for a good minute, and then, do you know what you did? You just turned around and left. I didn't see you again for the rest of the night. You just left!' There was clear protest and dissatisfaction in her voice.

'Are you serious?' *This was my crime?* 'Is this why you don't want to spend the night together?'

'Yes, Khaya! You and I are never going to get there ever again,' she said, her tone serious.

I felt like I was being given a life sentence for stealing a slice of bread. The punishment did not fit the crime.

'Really? Just because I left? I was completely out of it. You know how it is at X's birthday – I am the deputy birthday boy, and people kept giving me shots. I called an Uber and went back to my hotel. I didn't even stick around to say goodbye to people because I knew they wouldn't let me leave,' I explained.

'I don't care. It's never happening between us again.' Her smile returned, but she turned her body towards the bar to grab another sip of her drink.

It had been a month since that party, and she was still holding a grudge. I relented because I knew she meant it. We carried on with drinks, laughing and reminiscing. Occasionally, I'd say, 'Are you seriously going to punish me in Amsterdam?'

'Yes, you think I am joking?' she replied, laughing.

Around midnight, I left and she went to her hotel room. We planned to spend the following day together too. I was convinced she would relent this time – my charm offensive would render her defences weak.

The next day, the charm offensive was in full force. We laughed, and she held my hand occasionally. I could sense that the walls were breached.

We had dinner and went to another bar that night.

'Don't think I don't see what you're doing. It's not going to work. I am still mad, Khaya.'

'Are you seriously going to punish the both of us?' I asked.

'I am not punishing us; I am punishing you. I mean it. It will never happen between us again.'

She was serious, I went back to my hotel, alone in Amsterdam, both amused and impressed. Who knew that a kiss she enjoyed could backfire so badly?

The suitcase in Turkey

I seem to have an interesting track record with suitcases. They have a way of abandoning me, one way or another, only to find their way back. In *To Quote Myself*, I recount the story of a suitcase my mother had given to me when I left Mdanstane to study in Cape Town. It vanished for months, only for me to find it about 10 kilometres away after a series of unfortunate events.

There's another suitcase determined to create its own stories in my life – an orange one with grey zip tracks that I bought when I first realised that travel might be something I did more regularly.

On one particular trip to Turkey for a work conference, my beloved orange suitcase faced a series of traumatic events. My trip had been perfectly curated by Zelda, the assistant to the Integrated Marketing team at Coca-Cola. She had organised my flights and hotel accommodation and all was hunky-dory. I was due to connect in Dubai before arriving in Istanbul. Connecting flights are always a bit risky, and that's where the trouble began.

Everything seemed to be going smoothly until I reached the baggage carousel in Istanbul. I stood waiting for my suitcase, along with hundreds of other passengers. There's always a strange sense of superiority among those who receive their luggage first, as if they've been blessed by some divine luck.

The number of suitcases and passengers dwindled until I was the last person standing, still waiting for my bag. The carousel came to a halt, and it became clear my suitcase wasn't coming. I panicked – had my bag been left in Johannesburg or Dubai? I dreaded the idea of it being stolen or lost and untraceable. Suddenly, that roll-on deodorant and change of clothes I'd packed seemed extremely valuable.

I told my colleagues who were travelling with me that my suitcase had gone missing. They laughed and said something along the lines of: 'Of course it had to happen to you!'

I needed to find someone who could help. I approached an airport staff member, but my ignorance showed when I assumed he spoke English. The blank look on his face told me all I needed to know. I had wrongly assumed that everyone working at an airport must speak English.

Eventually I saw a baggage claim sign in English and followed it to a small office. The space had the bureaucratic air of a government office, not exactly inspiring confidence. The woman behind the desk had a friendly face, the kind that suggested she was well-practised in mothering but also knew where to draw the line.

I smiled and explained my problem: I had flown from Johannesburg via Dubai, but my suitcase had not arrived.

'Suitcase?' she asked.

I nodded.

'Lost?' she asked.

I nodded again.

'Colour?' she said.

I realised that she was using single English words. *The whole world doesn't speak English, Khaya*, I reprimanded myself.

We managed to communicate through a combination of gestures and very educated guesses. I filled out a form, and she handed me a colour palette. I pointed to the orange.

The airline promised to contact me the following day to let me know if they had located my suitcase. Thankfully, I was reunited with it two days later. I had resorted to using the hotel's roll-on deodorant, which I did not like very much. My colleagues, amused by the entire ordeal, decided that we should have drinks to celebrate the return of my suitcase.

On the day we were returning to South Africa, we were picked up in what looked like a delivery van that had been repurposed into a taxi. The friendly taxi driver loaded all our bags into the back, securing the doors that met in the middle.

We were in a bit of a hurry as the roads were notoriously busy at that time, the driver told us. He was right – the traffic was congested, not helped by the fact that the Turks seemed like crazy drivers.

Whenever he found a gap, the driver sped up on the highway. We were joking about the possibility of missing our flights. At one point, we got stuck in heavy traffic, but our fast-thinking taxi driver swerved into the emergency lane, accelerating quickly. Suddenly, we heard a loud thud and a scraping sound behind us.

I looked back and screamed, 'My suitcase!' Everyone turned to see it lying there in the middle of the highway. Due to the sudden acceleration, the doors had opened, and my suitcase had flown out the back of the van.

'Driver, please stop! Please stop!' He looked back and saw the suitcase too, now resembling some sort of art installation in the middle of a Turkish highway.

The car erupted in laughter. 'Of course, the only bag that would fly out of the car is Khaya's bag!' a colleague said, struggling to breathe from laughing.

Our driver braked hard. The suitcase was now at least 50 metres away. He apologised, reversed a little and then decided against it. Instead, he got out the vehicle and ran towards the orange suitcase to retrieve it. The laughter in the car did not stop.

My suitcase was placed safely back in the van, and this time, our driver made sure that the doors were secured. The only reason it hadn't been run over was because we were in the emergency lane, and no other cars were driving there.

The orange suitcase lived to see another day.

How many coincidences can a day have?

I first met Safiyah Vally at a wardrobe session for a Coca-Cola advert we were about to shoot. (A wardrobe session is when the cast of the advert assembles to review the outfits they'll be wearing on-screen, ensuring they align with the story being told and meet the brand's standards.)

At the time, I was the Senior Communication Manager for Content Excellence and Digital at Coca-Cola South Africa, and as such, I was responsible for overseeing strategy and creative work. This meant that I had to approve the cast, wardrobe, art direction, and sign off on the final product for any television commercial, print ad, or billboard campaign developed by our appointed agencies. Of course, I wasn't the sole decision-maker.

Saf soon became one of those friends where a year can go by without speaking, but then there are months when we speak every day and spend an inordinate amount of time together. She is also beautiful, with a ready smile and a dimple on her left cheek.

One day, when we both lived in Cape Town, she called me to hang out since we hadn't seen each other in a while. Being the nice and (almost) good-looking guy that I am, I decided to do her the favour of my delightful and charming company.

'Should we do The Athletic Club & Social at, say, 7 pm?' I suggested. She agreed that it was a good spot, and I told her that I would head to her place in an Uber. We could then go out together from her place.

When I got to Saf's place I told her about the amazing Uber driver I'd just met. He was Serbian. I'd never met anyone from Serbia.

Saf asked, 'Is his name Alexander?' I said yes. 'Oh my God, he also dropped me off an hour ago,' she said.

So I said, 'Was he driving a white E-Class?'

She exclaimed, 'Yes!'

We were highly amused at this small coincidence and shared our experiences of the Uber driver we were now calling Alexander the Great.

An hour later, I called an Uber to take us to The Athletic Club & Social.

Guess what? It was a white E-Class! I refused to believe that it could possibly be Alexander the Great from Serbia. I hadn't looked at the name on the app.

We got in and it was him! Together, we had now taken three trips with this man within a few hours.

After he dropped us off at the restaurant, I noticed a couple I recognised at a table of six people next to ours.

'No way,' I said to Saf. 'Those two guys were the previous tenants in the apartment I moved in to.' She couldn't believe it after the coincidences we'd already had with Mr Serbia. 'It's true! I met them when I first went to view it. In fact, they had this massive built-in bookshelf, and I asked them if they were going to drill it out from the wall because I'd love to have it.

They were happy to leave it for me – for a small fee, of course. The primary reason I chose that apartment was because it had a big enough shelf for my library of books – and it's only a seven-minute walk to my offices.'

I went over to say hi and introduce them to Saf, who started telling them about the odd coincidences we'd just experienced. When she mentioned the Serbian Uber driver they exclaimed, 'No way! Was he was driving a white E-Class? Because we also had someone from Serbia drive us!'

At this stage, we were all equally flummoxed. Alexander the Great from Serbia seemed to be the busiest driver in the land.

Saf then told them: 'I met Khaya when I was shooting a Coca-Cola ad. He was the client.'

One of them replied, 'Oh my God, you are so beautiful – we were looking at you before you came over and I just said you would be great for this Coca-Cola ad. We are looking for someone with your look.' They owned a casting agency. Saf and I had first met on the set of a previous Coca-Cola ad, and now, by chance, we'd crossed paths with people casting for another one.

It was a series of unbelievably serendipitous (I have never used this word in my life) moments. It had to mean something.

I don't know what it meant. Maybe coincidences are just coincidences – Saf didn't even get the Coca-Cola job because she didn't go to the casting.

The end.

The rugby team that harassed my friend

The more someone is uncertain of who they are and what they stand for, the more likely they are to resort to violence, seeking control in the chaos. This is particularly true for men, who often navigate a world where strength and dominance are prized. You don't need to be a man to know that even men are afraid of other men. There's a certain finality to violence – you either win or lose, strike or get stricken. Often, the mere threat of violence is enough to stop potential confrontation.

One night, I had an encounter where I feared I might be physically attacked. At the time, I worked for an advertising agency, MetropolitanRepublic, led by a high-energy gentleman named Paul Warner. He invited the entire creative department to attend what was known as the world's best design conference – the Design Indaba, held annually in Cape Town. The agency covered all our costs for flights and accommodation, flying us from Johannesburg to Cape Town.

During that time, I had developed a close friendship with a beautiful colleague named Cara. She was a Jewish woman with strong opinions, far more stubborn than her easy, ready smile

I turned the last flight of stairs and saw four massive guys in rugby uniforms, holding beer bottles. Two were leaning against the balcony, while the other two were near Cara's door.

They saw me, and I saw them. I began to walk up the steps with more certainty and authority than I really felt.

'What's going on here?' I said with the boldest, deepest voice I could muster.

I tried to sound as unintimidated as possible, but those guys could have kicked my butt and beaten me senseless. I walked up the stairs towards them as confidently as I could, but also slowly, making sure that there was enough distance between us if I needed to run.

Suddenly, they seemed uneasy. They shifted, their shoulders dropping.

'We are looking for our friend,' one of them said in a Spanish-sounding accent. This spokesperson was likely the best English speaker.

'Well, your friend is not in this room,' I said, as the two near the door moved away to join the others. 'Why have you been knocking for 30 minutes?' Silence.

'Try the next room,' I suggested, pointing to the only other door nearby. 'Go on, knock next door. Maybe your friend is there. What's stopping you?'

They looked at the floor sheepishly. By now, I knew I'd won the psychological battle. Whether it was because I was a scary black man or because they thought someone else was coming, they weren't going to fight me. I took the final step up and, feeling more confident, I told them to leave before I got them banned from ever coming to this country ever again. 'I suggest you leave now if you won't knock on the next door.'

When they were gone, I knocked on Cara's door and told

her it was me. She let me in and locked the door behind us. She looked pale, terrified. I hugged her and apologised for what she'd gone through. She asked me to sleep on the couch because she was worried the rugby players might see me leave and come back.

A few hours later, I woke up and went back to my room to shower. The whole party from MetropolitanRepublic was flying back to Johannesburg that morning.

When I got to the parking lot, the vans were waiting to take us to the airport. Cara was recounting her night of terror to everyone there, mentioning that she even had to ask me to sleep in her room.

When she finished, another colleague turned to me and, without saying anything, dramatically reached for my beard. He pulled out a long blonde strand of hair. Then another. When he was done, he said playfully, 'So you slept in Cara's room, hey?'

Umsebenzi

Every once in a while, there's an umsebenzi or umcimbi – a traditional ceremony – that, as a black person, you have to attend in a remote area. For many of us, that means leaving whatever city you now live in so that you can be present.

While I may not be a fervent traditionalist, I am steadfast in observing our culture and customs, and these ceremonies are important for bringing families together beyond Christmas, funerals, and weddings. They allow you to reconnect with relatives you hardly ever see and are a reminder of your roots, with cousins and their countless children running around, connecting you to your centre.

And then there are the uncles who have a close and persistent relationship with the bottle. You know the ones. When they see you pull up in your car from Johannesburg, they're ultra-friendly, reminding you how they used to stick fight with your father and what a great fighter he was – and how he would always give them money.

And of course, you play along. This uncle amuses you and you somehow miss him, even though you want to limit your interactions before he goes overboard. You know that the conversation will soon lead to him asking you to buy him a bottle of alcohol or hand over some cash. Even though you expected it, you also know he does love you – just not quite as much as he loves his bottle.

There is also always that cousin you don't trust around your belongings, because things tend to go missing when he's in the vicinity. You make sure you 'happen' to be in the room whenever he enters it.

And then there is the aunt who will go through your bags and help herself to things for her children because, as she explains, you work in Johannesburg, have money, and can spare these items. She'll remind you that when you were a baby, she used to carry you on her back when your mother was away. In fact, the way she tells these stories, it seems like a miracle that you did not come out of her womb.

These ceremonies can be for any number of occasions: a coming of age, the unveiling of a tombstone, or presenting a child to the ancestors.

Some people mistake these ceremonies for ancestral worship, but there's no ancestral worship in Xhosa culture. As my uncle, Mvume Dandala, a former bishop of the Methodist Church of Southern Africa, once explained: we don't worship ancestors; we venerate them. We recognise that they existed, that they were here before us, and that we wouldn't exist without them. It's a spiritual recognition of the continuum between the past, the present, and the future.

This time, I woke up early so that I could leave my apartment by 4 am and start driving from Johannesburg to Mount Ayliff. The advantage of leaving that early is that the roads are clear, with few obstructions for the first few hours. By the time there is traffic, you are already halfway there.

This particular umsebenzi or umcimbi was the tombstone unveiling of my Uncle Mavela's wife in Dutyini. I never knew her actual name because she was always referred as his wife or by her clan name, like many older people. Uncle Mavela Boyce had a gruff voice and had returned home after years of working in the mines in Johannesburg with a neck that was permanently stiff from an incident underground. I was often sent to his house as a young boy. He loved me dearly and never called me by my name, always saying, 'Mtshana wam' ('my nephew'). In English, 'my nephew' somehow feels diminished, failing to capture the closeness and affection it carries in isiXhosa.

On the day of umsebenzi, I noticed a group of women I didn't know fussing over me, making sure I was eating. They even dished up breakfast for me, serving the best ulusu (tripe) and umbhako (freshly baked bread) on an enamel plate. I assumed they were relatives who remembered me from childhood, because Lord knows, every msebenzi has one or two people who greet you with stories like, 'Don't you remember me? I am your aunt so and so,' or 'I used to carry you on my back,' or 'Oh my goodness, I remember you used to shit all the time and I changed your nappies.'

Yet these women offered no stories. I waited apprehensively for at least one of them to let me know how they knew me, but these women just continued serving me without revealing any information. You know when you get food before anyone else and you get the best parts of the meat? I was that guy. Ordinarily, my aunts or other relatives would treat me this way, but these women were strangers to me as far as I could tell. I was used to VIP treatment when going to umsebenzi of relatives, but this was a step up.

Eventually, one of them asked, 'Do you remember us?'

I panicked, thinking maybe I was wrong – maybe they were family members after all. I searched through the files in my brain, even the deleted ones. Still, I found no search results.

I finally said no, sheepishly.

'You gave us a lift yesterday to town from Dundee village. We were by the tarred road, hitchhiking, and you stopped your fancy car for us.'

'Owu, ndiyakhumbula!' I remembered.

I'd been driving from Johannesburg the day before and saw three women by the side of the road, waving down cars. I stopped and we first exchanged pleasantries.

'Molo,' they greeted.

'Molweni,' I replied.

They told me they were heading to town, Mount Ayliff, about fifteen minutes away, and asked if I could give them a lift if I was going that way. I said I was and invited them into the car.

As soon as we started driving, they spoke among themselves. 'Zange ndiyikhwele ke imoto enje.' ('I have never been in a car like this.')

Another added, 'Uyabona indlela ayivakali?' ('You know, you can't even feel the road.')

The third one then said, 'Ngathi yibhanoyi mntaka bawo.' ('It feels like you're on a flight.')

The other two laughed and roasted her: 'Wakhe wayikhwela phi ibhanoyi?' ('When were you ever on a plane?')

We eventually reached the town of Mount Ayliff and I dropped them off at the Menyo garage. They proceeded to heave themselves out, gripping the seats, doors, and handles, and grunting as they manoeuvred their way out of the car. When they offered to pay, I declined, saying I'd been headed that way anyway and wished them a good day.

I had not really paid attention to what they looked like once they were inside the car because I was focused on the road. So I remembered people who I'd given a lift to, but not their faces. If I had been asked to pick them out in police line-up, I would never have been able to.

They carried themselves with a certain rural teacher demeanour that I can't quite describe. I figured they must have been teachers; after all, many of my relatives in the Eastern Cape had taken up the profession, and there was a certain *teacherness* about them that felt familiar. I had been thoroughly entertained by their conversation in the car the previous day.

They called my aunt, who is a teacher, and began talking about me to her like I wasn't there, just like they had done the day before in my car.

'Yhu, unobubele lomntwana. Yazi usiphe ilift kula moto yakhe ingathi sisikhephe engasazi nokusazi, mahala futhi!' ('He's such a kind child. Imagine – he gave us a lift in his car that's like a boat, not even knowing us, and for free!')

'Kaloku abantu abaqhuba iimoto zesimanjemanje abasikhwelisi. Ikusikelele inkosi Madiba.' ('Nowadays, people driving these fancy cars don't give us lifts. Thank you, Madiba.')

And that's when I realised why I had been getting the VIP food treatment all morning. This wasn't just about the ride or the car; it was about gratitude and connection. That small act of kindness had resonated in a way I hadn't anticipated.

When we gather at these traditional ceremonies, it's never only about the rituals or the formalities – it's about the people. It's about reconnecting with one another in ways that go deeper than titles or roles, beyond who we are or what we do. These moments remind us of our shared humanity, our sense of connectedness, and the strength of our community.

Self-imposed mgowo

Some days feel like they were planned and executed by Satan himself, days when you're hit with one challenge after another. In isiXhosa, we call this umgowo – a state of going through the most, often because of life's relentless obstacles.

I had taken a flight from Johannesburg to Cape Town, where I now lived. When I landed in Cape Town, the weather was considerably European in its aesthetic: cold, grey, and wet. It had been a whirlwind of a weekend – I'd flown from Cape Town to Johannesburg, then Johannesburg to Durban, then back to Johannesburg, and finally from Johannesburg to Cape Town, all in a few days. I was looking forward to nothing more than napping on my couch when I got home.

I'd called an Uber to fetch me from the airport and the closer I got to home, the happier I became. I was even thinking about what snacks to have while watching TV under my duvet on the couch. I could already imagine the moment I'd arrive, put my bags down, and take off my shoes and pants – because home is where the pants aren't.

The Uber finally got me home. I opened the car door to get out from the rain as quickly as possible, grabbed my bag from the boot (or as our American brothers and sisters call it, the trunk), and walked up to my front door.

When I reached the door, I dislodged the backpack and began looking for my house keys. I could not find them. *Maybe I left them in the pants I was wearing the day I landed in Johannesburg*, I thought. I unzipped my bag and rummaged through my clothes, hoping to find the elusive keys.

No keys. Pants, backpack, suitcase. No house keys.

At this stage, I was concerned that someone might call the cops on me as I was standing there, clothes scattered around me, rifling through my bag like a madman. I even took on the universal 'thinking man's pose' – hands on hips, standing up straight, staring off into the distance as if perplexed and deep in thought.

Then, a new idea hit me: maybe I'd left the keys in my car in the garage. But then, the thinking part of my brain realised that couldn't be possible – I wouldn't have been able to close the garage door if the keys were inside the car. Meanwhile, the rain and cold were not being kind to me.

I stuffed my clothes back into the bag, resumed the 'thinking man's pose', and thought again. *Maybe the keys are at the Cape Town office?* That seemed likely.

So, I called another Uber. The office is no more than a three-minute drive from my place, or an eight-minute walk, but I was not prepared to drag my bags through the rain.

At the office, I used biometrics to unlock the front door and shot up to my desk upstairs. The entire place was empty, and after searching, I confirmed my keys were certainly not there either.

The 'thinking man's pose' resumed. I had a bright yet depressing thought – I must have left the keys in the office in

Bryanston, Johannesburg. It was the only logical conclusion left. I felt dismayed.

Dragging my bags, I went to the hotel across the road from the office, Stay Easy, where I often stayed when I was commuting between Johannesburg and Cape Town. I sat down in the lobby and curled up on a sofa. Just as I was considering booking a room, I had another idea: call my helper, who had a spare key. But there was one small problem: it was Sunday.

I agonised over disturbing her at home. Finally, I decided texting would be less intrusive. My helper is an older woman in her sixties, and I figured she might be at one of those church services that take a billion hours to end. I sent her a message, then waited. And waited.

After 100 billion hours, she called me. I'd been right – she was just leaving church.

'Molo, Khaya,' she greeted.

'Molo, Mama,' I replied. 'Could I ask a huge favour? I left my house keys in Johannesburg, and now I'm stuck at a hotel in Cape Town. I was wondering if I could use your spare keys to get in.' She agreed and I told her I was going to send an Uber to her address – she could pass the keys to the driver. I would let her know the car's make and registration once it arrived. I thanked her profusely.

I tracked the Uber as it made its way from her place to the hotel. After what seemed like several lifetimes, I finally had the keys.

I asked the same Uber driver to drop me off at home, adding the destination on the app.

Finally, I was home.

As I dropped my bags, I realised I was starving. I hadn't eaten all day. I decided to go buy isibindi. The place I buy it does not do Uber Eats so my only option was to drive. I needed comfort food after the three-hour ordeal I had just been through.

I stepped outside and opened the garage door.

No car.

I panicked for 0.05 seconds before remembering that I'd left my car in the parking lot of the hotel opposite the office. *The very same hotel where I'd been waiting for my house keys for hours!*

But wait, there's more. I also realised that my house keys had been in the car all along.

That Sunday, I went through self-imposed mgowo. Satan had nothing to do with it after all.

Near-death experience in the United States of America

Over the last few years, I've often found myself in the state of California in the United States of America. This time, I was staying in the Bel Air suburb, high up in the hills of Los Angeles. It's a green and leafy area, with rolling hills and palatial modern homes perched atop them.

One morning, after everyone had finished breakfast, I stayed in my room, still battling the last remnants of jet lag. I could hear a commotion down by the pool. My friends – Selebogo and Thabang Moalusi, Shyanne Valentine (an American friend) and my cousin Xolisa – were obviously having a pretty good time without me. Eventually, I managed to drag myself out of bed, open the curtains, then the sliding door, and step out onto the balcony.

On the grass near the pool sat a sweet-looking, inflatable golden swan – one you could easily mount and float on in the water. Beyond the edge of the infinity pool, the entire city of Los Angeles sprawled below, with a sliver of the ocean visible in the distance.

My friends were showing their private school swimming

skills. These were kids who clearly went to schools with lots of white people, where swimming lessons were compulsory.

'Must be nice!' I shouted down to them.

'Come! Join us!' they shouted back.

I was reluctant to swim, but I wanted to be part of the fun. I was still dressed in tracksuit pants and the T-shirt I had slept in. I made my way downstairs, past the kitchen and through the sliding doors to the pool, where my friends began cheering, trying to coax me into jumping in. Xolisa and Thabang were in the pool.

They kept urging me to join, but I'd deliberately come down without changing into swimwear to avoid getting in the pool. They were not having it. They wanted me in the water. 'Guys, I am not going upstairs to change and then coming back down here. But I will get on that swan,' I offered. They seemed happy with my compromise.

I wanted to be in the pool without actually being in the water. So, I poured myself a glass of champagne and basked in the Los Angeles winter sun. I even managed to mount the golden swan without spilling a single drop of champagne or getting wet. With my shades on, I felt like the coolest movie star in all of LA.

Naturally, the 'gram had to be appeased too. I needed to post evidence of my glamorous moment, complete with the backdrop of the glorious Los Angeles skyline. I commissioned Shyanne, who hadn't jumped into the pool yet (something to do with her hair not needing to mix with water), to be my unpaid photographer.

Floating with my glass of champagne in hand, and as Thabang hyped me up with shouts of 'King Khaya!', I felt carefree. It was all so Hollywood. But then I noticed something

– the swan was drifting towards the edge of the infinity pool. Slowly, but undeniably.

Using my elbow, I propped myself up, still carefully clutching the glass with my sparkly beverage in my right hand. 'Guys, I think this thing might float over the edge,' I said, trying not to sound too worried.

'No way,' Xolisa reassured me.

'Just paddle backwards,' Thabang suggested. I tried, using one hand, because I wasn't about to let go of my champagne. The swan, however, had no intention of slowing down or changing direction. It was headed straight for the edge, determined to see me dead.

'Guys, I am going to fall over the edge,' I said, this time more urgently.

'No man, don't panic, you won't—' But before Thabang could finish, I unceremoniously abandoned the swan and plunged into the pool, fully clothed. When I surfaced, the champagne flute was no longer in my hand.

As laughter erupted around the pool, I found the glass and scooped it out, while we all watched the swan continue its sinister journey towards the edge of the infinity pool.

Later, a debate ensued about whether or not I would have actually gone over. Everyone except Selebogo was convinced the pool's edge would have stopped me. Selebogo, even while laughing, agreed with me – jumping out was the right decision.

Later, an experiment was conducted on the swan, and it was determined that I would have floated over the edge. That part of the pool was built on stilts to accommodate the steep drop – a drop that would have been long and terrifying for this human being. Broken bones and deceasement (yes, it's a word now) would have occurred. All I imagine now is how my mother would have reacted if she were told how I died in America. She'd probably say, 'Ibiyi America etheni le ebesiya kuyo kuqala?' ('What was this America he went to in the first place?')

After saving myself from myself and swimming back from the deep end (yes, I can swim), I took a shower and went to look for my shades. They were nowhere to be found.

'Has anyone seen my glasses?' I asked later.

'Weren't you wearing them in the pool?' Thabang asked, convinced. I wasn't sure.

We checked the pictures and videos Shyanne had taken, and lo and behold, the shades were on my face while I was sipping champagne in the pool. But after my unceremonious dismount, they had vanished. We eventually found them at the bottom of the pool.

Looking through this footage on Shyanne's phone, I realised how dangerously close I had been to the edge before I decided enough was enough.

They say live life on the edge, but that was too close. Thankfully, I am a coward.

God's favourite, Job, and the weird office bet

Hardship can be viewed in many ways when we're confronted with it. Some see it as the end of the road, an insurmountable obstacle with no way out. Others view it as a test of character – a chance to reveal who we truly are in moments of trial. Do we succumb to our worst instincts, displaying the worst version of ourselves, or do we endure with the hope that something meaningful might come from the struggle?

According to the Holy Book, Job was the wealthiest man on earth. Not only did he possess an enormous amount of wealth, but he also seems to have been blameless in the eyes of God. This was a man who did not sin or offend God in any way. He had more camels, sheep, donkeys, and cattle than anyone else, and even more land. He was also a very fertile man, having sired ten children.

Please indulge me as I share my version of events, because the tone of my version is markedly different from that of the Good Book. Ready? Let's begin.

One day, the Devil challenged God, claiming he could make Job curse Him. The Devil believed that the only reason Job loved God was because of everything God had blessed him with. The moment God turned off the ATM of blessings and good fortune, surely Job would turn away from God and curse Him? Why would he still see good in God if he suffered despite being pure and blameless? Why would God allow misfortune to befall a good man?

Then God said, 'Are you sure, Devil, you son of gun?'

'You made me, so you can call me a son of whatever and see if I care,' Satan replied, rolling his eyes in exasperation. 'Thixo waseGeorge Gogh.'

For those who may have forgotten this iconic phrase in our nation's history, it came from none other than Jacob Zuma. During his presidency, Zuma provided us with many memorable and memeable moments. In parliament, Zuma was responding to repeated questions about Nkandla, and in a moment of visible exasperation, he rolled his eyes up like a teenage girl and said, 'Thixo waseGeorge Gogh' ('God from George Gogh'). We had never heard the expression, but it was forever etched in our memories from that day.

The dark prince continued: 'Of course it's easy for Job to love you when you've given him everything. What's not to love about you? He's clearly a fav of yours and he knows it. In fact, it's not much different from a woman falling in love with a rich man, only to leave him when things go south.'

'That's so sexist, bro. You could get cancelled for that,' God shot back.

'I said what I said,' the cheeky bugger retorted.

They went back and forth discussing the matter.

Eventually, God said, 'Look, I am confident in Job. There is no way he will abandon me. He worships me because he wants to – because he finds me to be his refuge and strength. So, do your worst, Satan.'

'Wow, hold up, God, are you saying I can do absolutely anything I want to Job to prove that he will curse you once he faces hardships?' the Devil asked, jotting down three sixes on a piece of paper. God, seeing this, casually placed three sevens on a slot machine.

'Well, you can do anything you want to him, except kill him,' God said while pointing a lightning bolt at Satan.

Satan put up his hands in mock surrender. 'Easy God, easy, I won't kill him. But I will certainly do my worst.' Hearing this promise, God put the lightning bolt away, saving it for a rainy day.

Once all the bureaucratic processes in heaven were complete and the documents signed, Satan unleashed hell upon Job.

While Job was relaxing by the pool, watching his stock portfolio rise, one of his servants rushed to him and said, 'The oxen were ploughing, and the donkeys feeding beside them, when the Sabeans raided them and took them away – indeed, they have killed the servants with the sword, and I alone have escaped to tell you!'

Before he had finished speaking, another servant came, saying, 'The fire of God fell from heaven and burned up the sheep and the servants, and consumed them; and I alone have escaped to tell you!'

While this second servant was still speaking, a third arrived: 'The Chaldeans formed three bands, raided the camels and took them away, yes, and killed the servants with the sword; and I alone have escaped to tell you!'

Finally, a fourth servant appeared, saying, 'Your sons and daughters were eating and drinking wine in their oldest brother's house, when a great wind came from across the wilderness, striking the four corners of the house, which then collapsed on them. They are dead; and I alone have escaped to tell you!'

At this, Satan let out the biggest villain laugh the world had ever heard. He turned to God and said, 'I didn't touch him, but everything he holds dear is gone. Now, let's wait and see.'

When the last servant told Job that all his children were dead, Job 1:20–21 tells us, 'At this, Job got up and tore his robe and shaved his head. Then he fell to the ground in worship and said: "Naked I came from my mother's womb, and naked I will depart. The Lord gave and the Lord has taken away; may the name of the Lord be praised".'[5]

'May the name of the Lord be praised,' Job said, even after losing everything, including his children.

His wife, however, had a more natural reaction. After the final straw – the loss of their children – she said to him, 'Are you still maintaining your integrity? Curse God and die!' In other words, what was the point of being good if you are still going to suffer? What is the point of it all then? It is a fair response.

But Job refused to curse God, saying instead, 'Shall we accept good from God, and not trouble?'

And God said, 'In all this, Job did not sin …'

And so, Job's story became one of the greatest tests of faith ever told. But if you ask me, it was also one of the most bizarre office bets in history. Either way, Job didn't curse God – and that's what mattered.

Job's story reminds us that life is rarely simple or fair. It is filled with moments that test the very fabric of our being, challenging our faith, resilience, and even our sense of justice. Resilience is not about denying pain or hardship – it's about finding purpose and meaning within it. Whether we see life as a series of random events or believe in a higher plan, what truly defines us is how we show up when the odds are stacked against us.

Nganga, the talented and capable

My younger brother, Nganga, was a very talented and capable person.

When I visited home during the holidays, when he was a little boy, I brought advertising award books with me so that I could go through award-winning ads. He'd see me poring over the clever print and billboard ads and reading radio scripts, and he'd pick up one of the books for himself to read. Soon, he'd be giggling and I'd quickly ask him what he was laughing at. He'd show me and I would marvel at how he could already catch some of the very clever ads at the age of ten.

Despite our twelve-year age gap, we were always close. I was a massive fan of the cartoonist Gary Larson. I'd buy his books and read them over and over again at home. My brother would sit next to me reading the abstract and often dark *The Far Side Gallery*. Everything I loved, he loved, so it was easy for us to get along.

I saw his creativity at an early age, so it was no surprise to me when he dropped out of what was then Peninsula Tech and decided not to pursue his diploma in event management. He wanted to get into advertising to become a creative.

He did not study advertising, but he had the ability to come up with a great idea – he had them all the time and he knew what a bad idea was too. He soon launched his career, working at agencies like Black River FC and MetropolitanRepublic, winning awards like a Loeries Gold and a Loeries Grand Prix.

Being in the advertising field was perfect for Nganga because his creativity was almost effortless; it flowed to and through him. Having worked in advertising for two decades myself, I have seen how some creatives can get into a rut and dread having to produce ideas again. But Nganga had a hack: to commit random acts of creativity. To limit creative endeavours to when you are at work makes the work of being creative a curse for some creative people. Nganga lived a creative life and was just always being creative, coming up with hilarious scenarios.

By the time he was hired by Catch + Release (the in-house communications agency for Rain, where I was the Chief Marketing Officer), Nganga had awards that most creatives in the country coveted. The ads that Nganga worked on suddenly gave the Rain brand a bit of an attitude and colleagues would come to me to say, 'Your brother worked on this, right? Because it has a charming attitude.'

There is no doubt that I was quietly proud of the fact that his voice and creativity were so apparent that others recognised them immediately. I had no doubt that he would surpass my own awards tally in no time, and I could not wait to see it happen.

'By the time you were my age, you hadn't won a Loerie Grand Prix like I have,' he'd say sometimes.

I'd retort, 'That may be so, but by the time I was your age I had my first Cannes Gold Lion. First!' We'd laugh and I'd joke he was bound to make great work because he had learned from me – his master. After all, the student must surpass the master at some stage.

In truth, though, he already had. He had practised advertising for such a short time yet achieved what many only dream of throughout their entire careers.

The problem with my brother

Two months before I lost my brother, I landed back in South Africa after spending two weeks in Los Angeles on holiday with my friends. It was January 2020, and after a few days in Johannesburg abusing my cousin Xolisa Dyeshana's hospitality, I headed back to Cape Town to get ready to return to work.

Nganga was then 29 years old and living with me. But when I arrived home, he wasn't there – he'd let me know that he was staying at a friend's place that night. My chance to brag to him about partying with Gabrielle Union, Dwyane Wade and The Weeknd on New Year's Eve would have to wait another day.

Feeling lazy, I put my bags down, looking forward to vegetating in front of my TV, perhaps playing a game on the PlayStation, and then going to sleep. But when I got to the lounge, I saw that my first-generation Apple speaker was not there. Then I began noticing that various other electronic items were missing, including the Apple TV, the PlayStation and the Wi-Fi router I had got from work. I decided it was a sign for me to go to sleep; I would ask Nganga where everything was the following day.

When I got up the next day, he was already out the door, presumably at work. It was very unusual for him to wake up and go to work before I did.

As I was leaving for the office, I received a text from him: 'I took the PlayStation, Apple TV, Wi-Fi router and Apple speaker to my friend's place while you were away. I was staying with him in December. He is in the Eastern Cape and he's coming back tomorrow. I will fetch them then.' I looked at the message more than a little irritated but held back and sent a thumbs-up emoji.

Tomorrow came and there was nothing.

I became increasingly agitated as the week went by. Nganga kept telling me each day that his friend would be back from the Eastern Cape tomorrow with my things.

When tomorrow came, the answer was again, tomorrow, and then another tomorrow. I was running out of tomorrows and patience.

I wanted to be kind and gentle, but I also wanted to be firm. I told myself that not being firm was being cruel. You can't live a good life avoiding consequences.

When it had been almost two weeks of tomorrows, I said to Nganga, 'I am giving you a deadline. If I don't have my things by Friday at 12 noon, I am going to call the cops. I am starting to think there is something you're not telling me ... Is there something you are not telling me?'

'No,' he said.

We were sitting on the couch eating dinner. Those days, the only time he'd sit on the couch with me was when the food from Uber Eats had arrived. He'd go back to his room not long after he'd taken his last bite.

'Nganga,' I said softly, despite having just made a threat. 'Are you in trouble?'

Looking away from me, he repeated, 'No,' with an uncertain smile.

'Nganga, if you're in trouble you have to tell me. You must tell me because I can't help you if I don't know. There is nothing you can't tell me.'

He was adamant that my things were with his friend and that I would definitely have everything back by Friday.

But the last tomorrow came.

At 11:15 on Friday, 45 minutes before the deadline I'd set, Nganga sent me a WhatsApp wanting to talk to me if I had time.

The message had undertones of 'I'm in trouble' written all over it, and I knew I had to brace myself emotionally. I needed to be a supportive older brother, no matter what he said to me. I said a little prayer to myself: 'Lord, be with me. Guide me. Help me make myself better than I am. Amen.'

This was not a moment for me to be my worst self. I had to face whatever he was going to tell me and make him feel safe, no matter what it was. Whether I was truly capable of this, I did not know. All I could promise myself was the attempt – because if I were the one in trouble, I would hope that the people around me would offer me the same grace.

My thoughts wandered in circles. *Could it be drugs? No, not likely. Maybe he needed money to party in December and to be as cool as the other kids who were buying bottles and having a good time, so he sold my items. Can't be it.*

I told him via WhatsApp to meet me in the boardroom where we both worked.

The room had lush, dark-grey carpeting and a long, dark, wooden table that occupied almost the entire room. The old wooden windows were covered by heavy, dark-green curtains.

He walked into the boardroom and sat down with a single, pastel-green chair separating us. I was ready for the worst, whatever it was. We were going to face this together. The things I had asked him about for weeks no longer mattered. I just wanted my brother to be okay.

'Sharp.'

'Sharp,' I replied, swivelling my chair to face him.

'What I am about to tell you is the worst thing you can possibly imagine.' He had thought about how he was going to approach this.

I remember thinking: *He wants me to assume the worst and when he tells me what it is, it won't be so bad.*

'It's really, really bad and it's been going on for a while.'

I kept quiet while he spoke.

'The truth is I have a gambling addiction. I can't help it; I just gamble all the time, and my salary is gone within days. So while you were gone, I took your things and sold them because I needed money. I am really sorry and so ashamed because you don't deserve this.'

I said, 'At least now we know what the problem is, and we can fight it. There is no need for you to keep it hidden in the shadows. This addiction relies on you feeling shame and hiding and pretending that things are fine when they are not.'

For a moment, I felt relieved, and my anger towards him lifted because I finally had information I hadn't had before. Yet I couldn't quite figure out what I felt right then. What he said didn't match any of the scenarios I had prepared myself for. I thought, *It's not that bad.* But the only reason I believed that was because I knew so little about what gambling does to a person – or to their relationships.

He looked down but I could see he was also relieved. The secret that had weighed on him so heavily was now no longer his to carry alone. He had given it up and resigned himself to the truth.

'Remember what I always say: "Never allow the illusion of desperation to cause you to make a decision you would never make"? Don't keep this to yourself. It's not so bad. I am here for you, and we will do everything we can to get you better. I know this was hard for you to say. Thank you for being honest and telling me. I knew you were in trouble, but I just didn't know what kind and I had to get you to tell me. Do you understand?' I said to him.

'Ewe, bhuti.' ('Yes, brother.' He always called me by the respectful 'bhuti' whenever he talked to me.)

We hugged.

He explained that he used a betting app on his phone and he bet on sports. I understood that gambling on his phone made it even easier for him because he didn't have to get up, draw money and then travel to somewhere like a casino. Gambling money via an app on his phone probably also meant that it did not feel like real money.

'We are going to beat this. Don't worry, we will concentrate on you getting better. It is okay not to be okay sometimes,' I told him.

We then spoke about the hard decisions and actions that were needed. I told him he needed to find a therapist. 'That will be your homework. I can't do that work for you – you must want to get yourself out of this.'

He agreed.

I raised my concerns that if things went missing at work, it would put me in a difficult position. I made it clear that I was not accusing him of this, but that gambling was a serious issue and since he had already pawned my electronics, I believed that we needed to add a precautionary defence in the workplace. We would need to tell the founders of each company about what Nganga was facing.

He nodded, saying he understood.

• • •

The goodwill that Nganga received from Brandon Leigh, the CEO and co-founder of Rain, and Craig Ferguson, the co-founder of Catch + Release, when they found out about his gambling addiction is testament to the respect Nganga had already earned and the genuine relationships he'd built.

This was a difficult personal matter, and I was grateful that we could speak about it openly. Nganga also confessed to them that he had in fact already pawned the company laptop and was going to get it back at the end of the month once he had been paid.

Though both Brandon and Craig were shocked and saddened, they were also incredibly empathetic. 'It's an illness, unfortunately, and it needs to be treated as one,' they said.

They both shared personal stories of their experiences with loved ones who had been in the throes of addiction and noted that the first step is admitting that it's a problem. They stressed to Nganga that the worst thing he could do would be to lie.

'If you want to get better, bru, you should know that this is not going to be an overnight thing. If you find yourself gambling again, you have to let Khaya know – or any of us. This addiction wants to keep you ashamed and hiding – but that way, you can't get the help you need. I promise you, bru, the best thing you can do is to be open and honest,' Brandon said to Nganga.

I thought they were extending Nganga a lot of grace in this situation. I told him, 'No one is going to punish you for backsliding, but we will for lying.'

His face was downcast, and his eyes were focused on the table. He appeared to shrink into the chair.

Trying to help

This was my brother. I loved him and was still proud of him. I feared and worried for him. How had I not known? How stupid was I not to have seen the signs? Was I so self-absorbed that I had missed this?

Nganga lived with me, and I did not see what I felt I should have been able to. We spoke every day. We laughed every day.

That previous November, we had sat on the couch watching rugby, hoping the Springboks would lift the Rugby World Cup for the third time – this time being led by the first black captain, Siya Kolisi. We'd laughed at a video of the victorious Springboks being welcomed by South Africans at OR Tambo International Airport. After noticing that Zozibini Tunzi was one of the esteemed guests, Siya Kolisi said, 'Hayibo, ayingoMiss South Africa lo?' ('Hang on, is this not Miss South Africa?') In December 2019, in the early hours of the morning, we watched Zozibini being crowned Miss Universe. We had never done that before, woken up for a beauty pageant, but we both had this belief – this wish – that she would win.

What were the signs that I had missed? I kept spinning.

While he was living with me, Nganga did not need to lift a

finger. I took him with me everywhere I went because I loved having him with me in Cape Town. If I was invited to a party, I often took him with me. In fact, the first time he met my friend Noni Gasa was when she had invited me to a party in a massive mansion in Llandudno where the drinks were flowing. If I was going clubbing, he was with me, and it was not uncommon for him to join me on dates too.

I had actually been secretly proud of him. A few months after he had moved from Mdantsane to Cape Town to live with me, he told me that he couldn't wait to buy a place of his own – that was his major goal. I kept that in my heart like a proud deputy parent.

I once asked him why he never had any money and what he did with it. He giggled and said, 'Stuff.' At the time, I thought that he just didn't want to say that he was saving to move out.

I believed that he was saving up so that he could become an independent young man. It kind of saddened me that he was going to leave me and not need me for anything, but I was very proud. I wished I had been the same at his age, and thinking about having my own place.

But then I also noticed that if I went out without him, he would have nothing to eat. He had no food unless I bought it. I had put it down to him just being a younger brother taking advantage of an older brother.

Now I realised this was a major clue as to the state he was in.

•••

After Nganga's confession about his gambling addiction, I told him I was proud of him for owning up. 'I can't imagine how tough it was for you to do.' I wanted him to be kind to himself, but I also told him he couldn't be slack. 'The long, hard road has to be walked, and it begins with tough decisions.'

I blamed myself for not forcing any responsibilities on him. All his money went to gambling. Perhaps with more responsibility, he would have felt like he was contributing to our family.

'You don't spend a dime in the house. I buy the food, I pay for the help, the electricity and when we go out, it's on me too. Here is what is going to happen: at the end of the month, you are going to start sending money home to our mother. It has been my sole responsibility forever, but we are both men in the Dlanga family now. I was sending money home when I was a waiter. All I could afford to do back then was to send home a few hundred rand a week so that you guys could eat and go to school. You have a much better job now than I did then.'

Over the next couple of weeks, I kept reminding Nganga not to be hard on himself, but to focus on getting better. 'You are going to beat this, Nganga.'

There was a vigour and energy in him during those days after the revelation, and I admired how he even woke up early and left for the office before I did. It was encouraging to see him that way.

But then I got a phone call from my mother two days after payday, asking me why I hadn't sent any money home yet.

Nganga had agreed to send the money, and I did not like the fact that my mother had to call me to ask. She also had responsibilities that she had to take care of.

At that point, I hadn't seen Nganga in three days, and he hadn't said where he was or what he was up to. Previously, I'd never worried when he was not around because I assumed he was with his girlfriend. But this time, I was concerned – he wasn't fulfilling the responsibility we had agreed on: sending money home. My calls to him weren't going through so I sent him a WhatsApp. I became increasingly agitated, concerned that he was backsliding into gambling.

I decided to check if there was anything missing at my place. There was – the Smeg kettle, a smart iron, my iPad, my AirPods Pro Max were all gone. We were back to square one.

Relapse

Nganga answered my text four days later, promising to fix things.

I was past being understanding and reminded him that all I'd asked for was honesty. 'Why can't you just be honest? Have you started gambling again?' My WhatsApp did not go through. 'It looks to me you wait for me to leave and then you come to the house and take what you want and then go off again.' This time the WhatsApps were read but when I tried to call the phone was off.

'Just so you know, there will be repercussions. I can't live with someone I can't trust in my own place.' I didn't have the heart to call the police on my brother but there was one thing I knew I could do no matter how much it hurt me. I was going to have to kick him out of my place.

• • •

That Saturday morning, I woke up angry, sad, and feeling guilty for even considering kicking him out. *Am I being my brother's keeper if I kick him out while he is in trouble? But if I let him stay, am I being an enabler? What is the right thing for me to do now? In fact, is there anything that's the right thing to do at this point?* I had no answers.

'I'm really sorry for everything I put you through. Not just for the past few weeks but your whole life. You never deserved any of it. You've been nothing but a good brother and role model and I have failed you time and time again. I'm truly sorry for that,' his WhatsApp to me read.

'The last person you have failed is me. You have failed yourself.' There was no grace in my message – I was fed up.

I was also scared for him. I had been asking him for two weeks now if he'd managed to find a therapist specialising in addiction and each time, he told me that he was still looking. I said to him, 'You need professional help. I will only help you if you are willing to help yourself.'

'I want to. I really do,' was his reply.

I went out with my friends that Saturday night, trying to forget my brother's demons that were haunting me, but he was not far from my mind because I kept checking my phone.

The next day, Sunday, he sent another text saying he had a confession to make. I was angry and felt betrayed. I'd given him enough chances to be honest.

He arrived at my place in the afternoon, averting his gaze and leaving a two-man-sized gap on the couch between us. He usually sat far too close to me and even closer when we walked on the streets.

'Hayibo 'fondi, do you have to walk so close that you push me?' I'd say to him. Sometimes I'd push him playfully because he'd walk so close that our shoulders would touch, and he'd laugh because he was doing it unconsciously. When he was talking and telling me some story, he would look down and push against me, lost in the story and just trusting that I was not leading him into some ditch. In many ways, Nganga had always been comfortable following me and leaning on me.

The things I had to say to him did not feel loving, but I felt they had to be said, and I knew they came from a place of love.

'I have been asking you for two weeks to find a therapist to help you. I told you if you find yourself gambling again you must tell me immediately. I gave you ample time to tell me and you didn't.'

'Sorry, bhuti. I know, bhuti,' he said. He told me that he had pawned the company laptop – again.

'I am only going to let you back here on condition that you start acting. I don't want plans – like planning to call therapists. I just want actions, Nganga. Then I will think about letting you back into my house.'

Later that afternoon, he sent me a message saying that on Monday, he was going to call rehab centres and find a therapist who specialised in gambling addiction. An hour later, he messaged me again to tell me that he was going to give me his phone so that he couldn't use the gambling app.

I was moved. I had not expected him to go that far.

Facing the fire

Monday morning was not a good morning. Nganga left for work before I did because I could not leave him in the house by himself and he knew it.

He also knew that he had to tell Craig about the laptop he'd pawned again.

After a number of meetings with colleagues, I asked Nganga if he had spoken to Craig, and he said he had. I then met with Brandon and Craig to talk about what we needed to do. I had already been in touch with Brandon the night before and he'd jumped straight into action, finding Nganga a therapist and offering to pay for him personally.

When the three of us met, we decided that we had to scare him enough to want to change and the best way to do that was to fire him. That, and get him to see a therapist.

I called him to meet us in the boardroom and outlined the consequences. He had been given a chance to be honest but now he could no longer be trusted with company equipment. 'You will fight this, and you will beat it, but for now, we can't have you in the office. You have been suspended with immediate effect,' he was told before being dismissed from the boardroom.

Brandon and Craig looked my way, not knowing what to say except sorry. 'This was very hard, bro. I don't know how you did it. I don't think many people would have dealt with this difficult situation with the wisdom you have.'

While I held what he said dearly, I doubted I had any wisdom. I could find no solace in breaking my brother's heart. I kept it together, nodding as Craig and Brandon tried to reassure me, but I was full of doubt. I imagined Nganga walking up Strand Street in the February heat, feeling the weight of everything, and I hoped I hadn't compounded any feelings of failure that he already had.

Brandon suggested that I tell Nganga what we didn't share in the boardroom – that we were actually going to give him three months off to get his act together. Once he was better, he'd be welcomed back but he would start from the bottom.

I ran out after him and saw him walking in the distance, up the slight hill on Strand Street. The sun beat down on me and the hot Cape Town air filled my lungs. He was walking surprisingly fast considering the news he had just taken in. I shouted his name, and he waited for me to catch up to him.

'Nganga. I want you to know that I don't hate you and that I am proud of you even though it does not look that way, but I am. No one hates you; you just need help. I am sorry this had to happen, but it had to be done. I honestly didn't know what else to do.'

'You had no choice, bhuti. I put you in an impossible position. I know that. You have done more than you should have. Please don't think I am blaming you for anything, this is all on me.'

We continued walking and I tried to catch my breath. 'What we didn't tell you is that we also decided to give you three months to get your act together. If you commit to getting better, you will be hired back again. You have not been abandoned; you have support and love.'

He said he knew that and wouldn't let me or himself down. He was determined to get better.

When we got to my place, we sat on the concrete chair on the patio and just talked as brothers. Despite the heat, he sat close to me, and I did not mind.

Hope pulled from under my feet

I had hope in my heart and I saw it in Nganga's eyes too. He was getting better, and we were having a good time.

We continued going out together. His situation didn't have to define who he was, and I still wanted him to enjoy himself, so I took him with me to places as usual. I did not want him to become a hermit or feel like a prisoner. I tried not to give him the time to spiral into self-flagellation.

I also didn't want to tempt him to gamble so I didn't give him money for food. Instead, I would get him Uber Eats. Every now and then he would feel like Nando's and we'd walk together to the Long Street branch to have lunch. When I was too busy at work, I'd let him use my Nando's Black Card – a special card given to me as a friend of the brand. With it, I could order Nando's for free at any store in the world. Fun fact: if you ask for one, you'll never get it. The only condition was that I could never tweet about it. I guess writing about it in a book now might break the rules, but it feels important to this part of the story.

That Nando's Black Card helped me immensely. It allowed me to feed my brother without giving him money, which was crucial in managing his access to money and helping him avoid the temptation of gambling. It also gave him a small sense of independence because he could walk into a Nando's and order his own food.

Every day before I went to work and when I got back, I would ask him the same question, and we both knew what I meant: 'Are you still strong?'

'Ewe, bhuti.'

He'd wake up and shower when I woke and get ready for his day outside the house. He even gave me a second phone I did not know he had.

He had no access to electronic devices that he could use to gamble. After a day or two of sitting outside my place, waiting for me to come home from work, he decided to grab a book from my long bookshelf and read to kill the boredom. He also started therapy.

'Listen, I am not a prison warden,' I said to him after a week of leaving him locked outside my house while I was at work. 'You will have to tell me that I can trust you. It is you who will say when I can allow you back in the house and when I can give you the keys and your phones. To be trusted is your responsibility, not mine. I will hear from you when you believe you are ready.'

'Ewe, bhuti.'

We lived without incident for three weeks, and he would give me feedback about his sessions with the therapist. The sessions were going well, but my Spidey-senses tingled one day when he told me that his therapist had complimented him about how well he was able to self-reflect, and that he seemed to be able to diagnose himself. That worried me.

Nganga's natural intelligence was unassuming – but if you

paid attention, you'd see how razor-sharp and incisive he was. *I think Nganga is playing this therapist,* I thought. *He has no idea how smart he is.* I thought he might need a new therapist but decided to wait and see how things went over the next few weeks. Perhaps I was overreacting.

Steadily, Nganga was regaining my trust, and I tested him bit by bit. My helper sometimes sent me messages about cleaning detergents she might need, so instead of buying them myself after work, I would give him cash to buy the items and he'd bring them back, including the change.

After a few weeks, he said he was feeling a lot better and asked for the keys and his phones.

'Are you sure you can trust yourself?' I asked.

'Ewe, bhuti.'

'Anything that happens with these now is on you. And you have to remember, if you fall back into the habit, you have to tell me as quickly as possible. You can't wait for days or for me to force you to tell me. Being honest and telling me is for your own protection.'

He said he understood and we left it there.

Not long after that, he did not come home one day. I asked him where he was via WhatsApp and he responded hours later saying he was at his girlfriend's place. He did not return the next day either.

When I got back home on the third day there were several items missing. I had given him access, given him keys to my house and returned his phones. I'd made a mistake.

The last time I saw my brother alive

Not again. This time I felt wounded by Nganga – I had thought that we were in a good space; he knew that he had the freedom to fall but that he needed to communicate with me if he did. That was the only requirement I had. He had to tell me.

I did not call or text him again. I wanted to give him a chance to come out and tell me that he had started gambling again. He knew the consequences of hiding it and I hoped that I was not going to have to kick him out again. Perhaps he was trying to gain the courage to face me, and I wanted to clear a path for him to do so by giving him the time.

He did not come home on Monday.

He did not come home on Tuesday.

He did not send me any messages to tell me he had fallen off the wagon again. I thought I had given him time to come out and be honest with me. Now I was mad.

He came home on Wednesday.

I heard the keys clinking as he opened the door. He walked in and greeted me, but I couldn't look at him. I could only bring myself to respond once he had walked past me and the television.

He went to his room for some time, and I was hoping he was trying to figure out how to tell me that he'd got lost in the darkness of gambling again.

He'd been hiding for an hour when I realised that he had no intention of coming out.

'Nganga!'

'Bhut'am!' ('My brother!')

'Yiz'apha.' ('Come here.')

'Ewe, bhuti.'

When he emerged from his room, his face was heavy, his eyes were red.

'Why do I have to ask you where my things are?'

His response was silence, and a thick wall of air seemed to rise between us. I held the silence, hoping he would volunteer what we both already knew. Even the sound of the television felt muted, blocked off by the tension in the room.

I told him that I'd said nothing for days while he was gone – I was hoping he would come out and say that he had fallen back into gambling so that we could work it out. He knew what my rule was: I just needed him to tell the truth. I did not expect him to be cured overnight. But I expected him to be honest.

He just stood and listened to me.

I told him that I was travelling to Johannesburg the next day, Thursday, and would be back on Monday. I'd have to kick him out because I couldn't leave him alone in my home again.

He said he was sorry.

'I don't need your apologies,' I told him. 'I want your honesty.'

Thursday morning came. The first thing I did was knock on his door.

'Nganga! Nganga!' I banged and shouted louder than I usually did.

'Bhuti!' he responded quickly. He unlocked his door, and I looked at him to make sure that he was fine. He seemed fine to me. I wanted to hug him and tell him that everything was going to be okay, but I didn't. I didn't.

I thought it would help him, motivate him, to see my anger instead of my love for him. I regret it. I do.

I told him to shower and get ready because I was not going to leave him in my house.

When we left the house that morning, I told him I'd heard from his therapist that he hadn't shown up for his session for the first time. I asked him to promise me to see the therapist. I also gave him R500 for food. I didn't want to give him too much money because I believed he would find a way to gamble with it, but I also wanted to make sure that he had enough to eat until I got back from Johannesburg.

I was going to be back on Monday, and I already knew I would take him back into my home again – but he did not know that. My plan was simple: since therapy didn't seem to be working, I would send him back to the Eastern Cape. Not back to my mother in Mdanstane, but all the way to the village of Dutyini in Mount Ayliff. I didn't want him to know my thoughts just yet.

At the airport, I spoke to my mother on the phone. She said I had done the right thing. I shared my plan with her, and she agreed it might be the best way forward. She reminded me of a time she had sent him to the village for six months when he was struggling to find work and spent all day in his room. 'Maybe this is the lesson he needs,' she said.

I felt reassured but I was also uneasy.

Finding out I'd lost my brother

I have always strongly believed that no matter how dark the times, there is always something, even briefly, that can bring a flicker of happiness. It was hard to be hopeful, but I had to carry on with the last fumes of willpower I had in me.

That day, I was at Joe Public in Bryanston, Johannesburg, sitting for a podcast with Loyiso Madinga. He still had the same boisterous laugh he'd always had.

I first met Loyiso when we both worked for Metropolitan-Republic. He was very talented and had a curious energy, often bursting into song.

With him in the boardroom at Joe Public was Tats Nkonzo. I had also known him for some years. They are both professional comedians and have featured on Netflix specials. Above all, they happen to be isiXhosa speakers from the Eastern Cape province, like me.

During the podcast, we were talking about family and I found myself turning to them for advice because I wasn't sure about what I had done. I was unsure and uneasy. My brother, I told them, has a gambling problem. I have spoken to him about it.

They assured me that the decisions I had made were the

right ones, that he did need some tough love to help him turn his life around.

The podcast recording ended, and we said our goodbyes. I left them in the boardroom because they had to pack up their equipment. As I opened the door to get out, I switched my phone back on and saw that I had a missed call from my sister, Siki. I called her back.

'Umama ufuna ukuthetha nawe.' ('Mama wants to talk to you.')

She handed the phone to Nolulama Mshumi, my mother's sister (we call our aunt Mama, while our mother is Anti – aunt).

'Nganga passed away at Groote Schuur Hospital in Cape Town this afternoon. I am so sorry. All I want to say to you is that you did everything you could to help him. You went far and beyond what a brother should do. There was nothing more you could have done,' she said.

It was not a phone call I was expecting. I felt blood rushing through my body. Nganga had taken medication that is prescribed to me and ingested all of it.

I found myself thinking about Job a lot

There is a soundless gong that goes off in your head when you find out about some deaths. The shock feels like it all happens between a dream and reality.

In the book of Psalm 138:3, King David writes, 'When I cried out, you answered me, and made me bold with strength in my soul.'[6] I cried out into myself that day. Tears are our sincerest prayers to God when we don't know what to say to Him.

The tears cascaded down my face. My eyes stared blankly into an abyss of nothingness. Every emotion I had ever known collapsed into itself, giving way to a new and overwhelming feeling – one I had never known before and could not contain.

I found myself thinking about Job when I went upstairs to my hotel room later. The story of Job is found in the Old Testament. It is a difficult book to understand and to accept because of the undeserved suffering that Job endures.

While I was not comparing myself to Job in any way, I did think: *Who am I to be angry at God if Job endured calamity after calamity but did not lose faith nor give up?* I had to find a way. The loss was so painful, I could not wrap my feelings around it.

I thought I could pray but I could not reach out and grasp God to ask Him for comfort. All I could think to ask God for was for some relief for my mother and sisters.

My grief clothed me in a heavy, suffocating silence. In those hours, alone in my hotel room, clothed in my grief, all I wanted was quiet. I switched off my phone for a while.

I wanted to pray but there were no words to say as I tried to sleep. I lay there, desperate for rest, for some respite from the new unknown aching of the soul.

In the book of Job 2:11–13, it is written, 'When Job's three friends ... heard about all the troubles that had come upon him, they set out from their homes and met together by agreement to go and sympathize with him and comfort him. When they saw him from a distance, they could hardly recognize him; they began to weep aloud, and they tore their robes and sprinkled dust on their heads. Then they sat on the ground with him for seven days and seven nights. No one said a word to him, because they saw how great his suffering was.'[7]

Job's friends sat on the ground with him for a week. With not a word. They were just there. It is a verse that has always puzzled me. I wonder about the silence. What must they have been thinking? Was he so downcast that they did not know what to say to him? Did they just look at him, then glance at each other and feel so overwhelmed that they just shut up? Silence while a friend is grieving is difficult.

The first thing we tend to do when someone has experienced a loss is dispense words of wisdom, encouragement, optimism – when all that's needed, often, is just the knowledge that you are there. The things that are said all begin to sound the same and generic.

Words like, 'It will get better with time' or 'Everything happens for a reason' get thrown around. These words are meaningless to the grieving, no matter how well-intentioned they may be.

I never understood why Job's friends sat with him in silence for seven days until I lost my brother. All you want is the presence of your people.

When South Africa's first democratically elected president, Nelson Mandela, was locked up on Robben Island, he got news that his first-born son had died. In his book, *Long Walk to Freedom*, he described:

> I do not have words to express the sorrow, or the loss I felt. It left a hole in my heart that can never be filled.
>
> I returned to my cell and lay on my bed. I do not know how long I stayed there, but I did not emerge for dinner ... Finally, Walter [Sisulu] came to me and knelt beside my bed, and I handed him the telegram. He said nothing, but only held my hand. I do not know how long he remained with me. There is nothing that one man can say to another at such a time.[8]

When Walter Sisulu saw how great his comrade and friend's grief was, he could not speak; he could only feel for him. He did nothing but hold his hand.

Job's friends dropped everything for him and said nothing. After seven days, Job finally spoke to his friends. None of them broke the silence until he opened his mouth – only then did they speak.

Silence can often be the most eloquent thing we can say to a grieving friend.

Friends like these

As soon as I heard the news of Nganga's death, all I could think was that I had to be the man of the house. I had to act and make things happen. I had sent money home to prepare for the guests who would want to be home with the family. I was meant to fly back to Cape Town on Sunday but changed my flight to Saturday morning. I had to go to identify his body and then move his body from Cape Town to East London. There was a lot that needed to be done.

On Friday night, I decided to text some friends to let them know that I had lost my brother because I did not want them hearing from others or finding out on social media.

I woke up on Saturday morning readying myself for the dreaded flight back to Cape Town. My phone rang and it was Shaka Sisulu, a big friend. He is a very tall man who is used to being the tallest person in most rooms. But his personality is even larger than he is and his friendship has come to mean a lot to me.

After extending his condolences, he asked, 'How are you getting to the airport?'

'I will drive myself there. I've got a rental.'

'Nonsense, you can't be driving yourself to the airport. For what reason?'

'Because I have to drop off the rental. The car can't drive itself there.'

'You're not going to do that. I am coming. I will pick you up and drop you off.'

'But I have to take the car to the airport.'

'That's fine. My brother will drive behind us to drop off the car.'

He countered every argument I was making. He was not having it. By the time I was done getting ready, he was already downstairs, waiting with Duma Sisulu, his brother. He got out of the car to embrace me with his large and comforting frame.

I remember my very first encounter with Shaka at a bar in Johannesburg. 'I like you. I think you are smart, but I don't like your politics.' Those were the very first words that this tall, dark and charismatic man said to me.

After telling him that I didn't have a political home, I asked him what his name was.

'Shaka Sisulu.'

'What? You can't be serious.'

'I really am,' he replied with a slight smile, and I couldn't tell if he was saying it to get a reaction out of me.

'As in Shaka Zulu and Walter Sisulu?'

'Yes, I was named after Shaka Zulu, and my grandfather is Walter Sisulu,' he replied.

'That is the most apt name I have ever heard.'

And on that day, our friendship began.

I handed the car keys to Duma and I climbed in the front seat with Shaka. He was in shock. A month before, I had called Shaka and told him about the problems my brother was having with gambling. I told him that he was going to therapy. On our drive to the airport, I gave him a brief rundown of the events leading up to my brother's eventual demise. I also realised that Shaka had taken the very last photo that I have of my brother and me together. He'd been in Cape Town in November 2019 and had insisted on taking a picture of Nganga and me. It's a terrible picture and he should never consider taking up photography, but it is special to me.

Shaka dropped me off at the airport and I caught my flight to Cape Town, sitting in the second row by the window.

After the plane was in the air, a wave of emotion from a bottomless dark ocean bubbled up. I took off my yellow Puma hoodie (which had the text 'Make things cool but worse' repeated as a pattern) and put it back on, but back to front. The hood was now covering my face.

The tears were unyielding, gushing from my eyes. Fortunately, there were no passengers next to me. I did not want to feel this feeling. The last time I saw Nganga I was mad at him. I cried because I was angry at myself now, questioning the decisions that I'd made.

There was an announcement about landing in Cape Town in the next 20 minutes, so I had to get myself together. I stopped crying and made sure that the tears were done. At least for now.

As soon as the wheels touched the tarmac, I turned my phone on and saw a message from my friend, Noni Gasa. She had defied me. I'd told her that I was going to Uber from the airport. Noni said she was not going to have me by myself after hearing such tragic news. She was going to pick me up with another friend, Sindiswa Ndlovu. I had no choice and at the time, I was incredibly annoyed by this invasion of my grief. I could not wallow in self-pity in an Uber by myself.

After disembarking, I stepped out of the airport to find Noni and Sindi standing next to Noni's car. I cannot begin to explain the relief I suddenly felt when I saw them. The hugs they gave felt like sponges sucking some of the pain away.

They put my small carry-on bag and backpack in the boot, and I sat at the back of Noni's car as an overwhelming sense of relief continued to descend over me.

I did not need to be alone. I needed to be with friends who cared for and loved me.

'I'm so sorry, my friend,' Noni said. 'But there is no way we were going to let you get an Uber home from the airport when we are here. What kind of friends would we be if we can't be here for you at this time?'

'You know what? I am so glad you did not listen to me. You guys picking me up is what I didn't know I needed. I'll be honest, I was so mad at you guys for being so persistent. In fact, I think I was determined to sulk once I got in the car.' We all laughed.

I had also received a text from Brandon. He asked if I was okay with him having reached out to our colleagues from Rain, and Catch + Release, asking them to come to the office around lunchtime after I landed. He said we could sit at the bar together, remember Nganga, and support each other. It was deeply touching to see how everyone had dropped their plans that Saturday to show up for me, for us, for Nganga.

As I arrived, I found not only my colleagues but also my friends like Noni and Sindiswa, Raine Michel, Kwakho Gongqo, and Kaone Kairo. Somehow, they had heard about the gathering and decided to be there too. The office, often a place of routine and deadlines, became a space of shared solace that day. That afternoon was about the quiet ways people hold each other up

Life is like that sometimes

when the world feels like it's falling apart.

A few years later, when I returned to the office after losing my mother, Gaba Guliwe wrote me a heartfelt card and condolence message that I hold dear. He did not just see a colleague who had lost a parent; I think he imagined what it would be like for himself. That card reminded me that grief has a way of connecting us in unexpected, deeply human ways.

That evening, after the gathering for Nganga, Xolisa flew from Johannesburg to be with me. He never left my side while we were planning the funeral. Anything I needed done, he did. He never tried to comfort me with any words – he was just there, like Job's friends.

The suicide note

Most days, I parked my car inside the narrow garage of my apartment building. The walls were so close together that if I had a passenger, they needed to get out before I parked, otherwise neither of us would be able to open a door. Parking was an act of precision, with the ever-present risk of scraping the car against the walls or the narrow garage door entrance. I'd done it before.

But that evening, I couldn't be bothered. I left the car on the street, too drained to manoeuvre into the garage.

The Cape wind was relentless, howling as I stepped out of the car and opened the gate leading to my small patio. My attention was suddenly drawn to the flapping and thrashing of book pages on the white concrete bench near the glass door to my bedroom.

I took a few steps towards the bench, and dread followed me before I could even pick up the Moleskine notebook. I didn't need to see what it was to know. I just simply knew.

On the bench, alongside the book, were coins, as if someone had bought some items, received change, and left it behind on the bench. Scattered around were orange plastic Bic razors.

The scene felt surreal. I knew what I would find in the pages of the Moleskine. Knowing didn't mean I wasn't in denial.

The razor blades were haphazardly placed, a couple lying on the ground, perhaps blown off by the wind. The coins, however, were neatly stacked. The Moleskine was open, its pages caught in the wind, battling for supremacy. I could see that some were written on.

I gathered all the items in the darkness on the bench, refusing to read the note just yet. Besides, it was too dark and windy to read outside on the patio. Too dark to read what I already knew. Unlocking the door, I placed the notebook, the coins, and the razors on the kitchen counter. I needed a moment.

I delayed by going to the bathroom. Standing there, I wondered: *Will the answers be in those pages? And will I even want them if they are? Will the answers give me the impossibility of closure?*

I went back to the kitchen and inspected the coins. They totalled R5.40, four one-rand coins, two 50-cent pieces, and two 20-cent coins. I placed them on the TV stand for reasons I couldn't explain, as if by doing so, I might shift the weight of their significance. The razors I put away in the mirrored cabinet above the bathroom sink – the one Nganga used.

Finally, I rested my elbows on the kitchen counter and picked up the Moleskine. My body felt like ice, and tears welled up before I even opened it. My guilt, which had been buried for a few hours by the busyness of identifying his body, going to the hospital where he had passed away, and going to the police station, threatened to erupt. *Am I about to find confirmation of what I feared most? Is this note going to confirm that I pushed him to his limit?*

The last letter Nganga wrote was addressed to me, and to

the family, but mostly to me. Even now, I can't think about it without guilt creeping in, though I know it has no rightful place.

In his letter, he apologised for what he had put me and the family through. He said he knew that I did all I could possibly do to help him and went beyond what I should have done. He wrote that he knew I loved him. He knew we all loved him.

But, he said, it was his fault. There was nothing else anyone could have done.

He admitted that his choice would cause us enormous pain, but he believed he was sparing us the persistent pain he had been putting us through with his addiction. 'You will feel pain one last time,' he wrote, 'and no more.' He said he loved us, apologised again and requested that we cremate him.

Pain, one last time? That was my first reaction upon reading his words. *Does he not know that this pain is everlasting?* Even then, I knew it would never end.

His pain and despair lay on the pages before me, as raw and final as his decision. I felt so very sorry for him. I wished he had not given up on himself – because we hadn't, and we never would. But in his mind, there was no other way.

Loss in the time of Corona

A few days before Nganga took his life, President Cyril Ramaphosa went on national television to announce that gatherings of more than 100 people would be illegal. This meant funerals too. And so, with the help of Xolisa, I had a funeral and a memorial service to organise under these new rules.

I did the things that life demanded of me. Not because I was ready, but because I had to. Funerals need planning in the middle of your emotions. Life is messy. It's a relentless battle of finding air before being plunged back into the deep. It's about surviving the waves as they come, one breath at a time. And yet, we fight. We endure. Because somehow, in the chaos, we learn to find fragments of temporary strength. And that is enough to carry on.

Nganga's memorial service was held in Cape Town because that's where he lived and worked. Hillsong Church in Century City generously offered to livestream the service, and they counted each person walking in so that we didn't exceed 100 people.

On the day of the memorial service, I cried in the shower.

After putting on my suit and a tie, I knocked on Nganga's door and opened it. I suddenly remembered that I could no longer ask him if he thought the suit looked fine or if I should wear another tie. That hit me hard. I was going to his memorial service, and I wanted to ask him what he thought of my outfit. It was as if for the first time, I understood that he was really gone.

At the memorial service, we practised social distancing, and it was almost amusing to watch people use the elbow greeting or wave to others, yet still feel compelled to hug me, my mother and sisters. There is a human need for physical touch with people who have experienced loss.

The funeral service we held later in East London was even stranger. Because of the new laws, I asked people not to come, to come only if they had to. Asking people not to attend a funeral was a first. The family prayer service felt even more sombre because there was just family, save for a few people from my mother's church.

At the Christian Centre in East London, we could allow more people without breaking any laws. The service would be streamed live to three different auditoriums in the centre, with family and friends housed in the main auditorium. Each group of a hundred people used a separate entrance, so they didn't congregate together.

Once we got to the church, I stood at the door, counting the number of people coming in the one entrance. I had to allow the elderly and family in first. You can just imagine some of the looks I was getting from certain members of the community who had come to support us. I was standing there preventing people from entering to provide us with support.

During the service, because everybody sat so far apart from

each other, it felt odd and cold. My mother was a lonely figure, sitting by herself with no one to comfort her. She occasionally hunched forward, her back so bent that her head was almost on her knees. I couldn't bear to see her like that. I saw the confusion around, people not knowing what to do, whether to go to her or not. Ordinarily, her sister would have been right next to her, holding her and stroking her back. But these were not ordinary times.

I picked up my chair to sit next to her and started stroking her back. My sister Siki then joined me.

...

In the weeks that followed, I was alone at home, without Nganga and without any friends or family because the country was under lockdown. Nganga had lived with me for almost a year.

I had never really known loss like this. I'd lost my father just before my sixth birthday – I was too young to know what loss was. Besides, I did not have a relationship with him. When I lost my grandparents, they were already old, and I had expected it.

I tried to avoid going into Nganga's room, but I saw it every day. I never closed the door. I was haunted every evening when I went to the kitchen to take my medication. I'd see him again in the empty containers of the pills he'd taken to end his life – the life that had given him a pain so great, he could not share it with me. I couldn't bring myself to throw the empty bottles away.

During lockdown, when I switched on Netflix, his name and avatar appeared next to mine on the screen. When he was living with me, he'd always be watching some random programme I had never heard of. I thought of those evenings in February when our eyes stared at the television we were not watching. It had served as a helpful distraction when things were difficult. We each had different points of pain, but we were also stuck together. At the time, it had felt like we were taking the difficult walk separately but together.

South Africa's Covid restrictions also meant that there was no Uber Eats and I had to cook – something I hadn't done in over a decade. One morning, I was making breakfast while naked because I was lazy and alone. Some of the oil landed on my ever-increasing mid-section and I felt some furious droplets landing further down. I jumped away immediately, yelping, and found myself shouting out to my deceased brother: 'If you were here, I wouldn't be naked with cooking oil burning me! Damn you!'

I had many random, seemingly ridiculous but really grief-stricken moments when I thought of Nganga, what he would have been doing, or what we would have been doing together.

Ironically, he had been a constant feature in the house and now that he was gone, I saw him everywhere. I was alone but he was still always there.

Mother's letter

Traditionally, when parents have lost a child, they do not speak at the funeral. They write a letter, which is read by a family member chosen to stand in their place. My mother, as much as she secretly enjoyed the attention she received while telling stories 'reluctantly' to family members, hated the spotlight when it was forced upon her. This was one of those moments.

Sis' Ondisa Dlanga, my father's youngest sister, was asked to read my mother's words. Written in isiXhosa, it was read aloud at the memorial service:

Nganga wabantwana, Ngangalala yam.
Ngangamsha yesixeko, samaDiba.

Hamba kakuhle Besh my son. Hamba kahle
seuntjie wam. Uyathandwa ngumamakho.
Ubukude nam, useseGoli ungathandi
kundifowunela nokuWatsappa de kube
ndim endikuzamayo. Usuke undixelele
u'ba uzakuthetha uthini. De ndayiqhela
ke loo nto yokunganxulumani nam. Ubusazi

u'ba mhlawumbi ubusazi u'ba sizokwahlukana
msinya ungafuni kundivisa intliziyo ebuhlungu.

Ubuthandwa ngabantwana bakokwenu bencoma
yonke into ngawe. Kodwa lento yenzekileyo
khange isithele kum. Bendithi xa ndivuka
ndichwechwe ndikukrobe uba ukhona usaphila.
De ndithume noSiku xa sihleli akujonge u'ba
uright na eroomini.

Wandibuza uSiku yintoni le nto ndisoloko
ndikhathala ngawe ndiyakufekethisa. Ndamxelela
uSiku u'ba andikuqondi ingathi ungazibulala.
Kanti kuzakuba njalo.

Hamba kakuhle Dlanga lam, hamba kahle
Gidi gidi Mthombo, dib'indonga zamaDiba
akuBhongela. Hamba maBhaku kaTat'omkhulu.
Wayekubiza Mabhaku ngenxa yeendlebe
ezinkulu.

Apha ekukhuleni kwakho simane sigoduka
utat'omkhulu wakho ekubuka nobuhle bakho.
Andicele u'ba ndimnike akukhulise ukwenzela
akuqinise.

Ungavumi usithi utat'omkhulu uyabhomba.

Ubuclever kakhulu bayakwazi abantwana
bakokwenu ububasolvela into emxakile lula nje.

Life is like that sometimes

Lala uphumle Diba udiniwe uxhwalekile
ziintlungu zomhlaba.

Here is my translation:

Nganga, my Ngangalala. My Ngangamshe of the Diba clan.

Go well, my son. Go well, my young son. Your mother loves you. You lived far from me and you didn't call me much even when you still lived in Johannesburg. When I'd ask why you were not calling, you'd say, 'But what will I say when I do call?' I eventually got used to you not contacting me. Perhaps a part of you knew that we would part ways soon enough and didn't want to leave me with a broken heart.

Your siblings loved you very much and they were always complimenting everything about you. But what has happened was not completely hidden from me. When you lived with me last year, I would wake up in the mornings and creep towards your room to see if you were still alive. I would even send your sister, Siku, to check up on you.

Siku asked me what is this. I always care about you. I call you names I would say to her I was unsettled because I felt you would take your own life. As it turned out, it would be so.

Go well, my Dlanga, go well, Gididi Mthombo, di'bindonga zamaDiba akuBhongela. Hamba, maBhaku kaTat'omkhulu. That's what your grandfather called you – maBhaku, because of your big ears.

Your grandfather would look at you and compliment your beauty as a child, but he was worried that you would grow up to be a soft child. He wanted me to leave you with him in the village so that he could raise you and strengthen you. When I told you, you would not because your grandfather was too strict and shouted a lot. You were too clever, your siblings knew this as you used to easily solve their problems.

Sleep well, Diba. You are tired. The pain of this world has exhausted you.

I had read the letter the day before, when my mother sent it to me as if seeking my approval, but it hadn't hit me as painfully then as it did when I heard Sis' Ondisa read it at the church. When I was reading it, it felt like just another item on the long list of funeral logistics I was trying to manage. I was focused on ensuring everything ran smoothly – confirming the order of events, meeting the deadline for the crematorium, and navigating the new rules that Covid had imposed on mourning.

Funeral services in the Eastern Cape are notoriously long, but now grief had a time limit. I was caught up in the whirlwind of planning, and my mother's letter became just another thing to check off the list. Perhaps I wasn't ready to feel its weight.

But as Sis' Ondisa read my mother's words aloud, something shifted. Her quiet acceptance struck me. Her grace moved me, even as she tried to bury her face between her knees while listening to her words being read out to the congregation. In that moment, my mother taught me something profound about love.

Love does not fight for control over another's pain. It does not demand answers or explanations when none can ease the ache. Love holds space for the unthinkable and for the choices that break us.

The letter wasn't just a goodbye to Nganga. It was a confession of the depth of her understanding, the breadth of her compassion, and the weight of a mother's unconditional love. She did not try to rewrite Nganga's story, nor hold him back from the peace he sought, nor judge him for the choice he made. Instead, she honoured his pain and the decisions that had brought all of us to that church. It was a grace I had not expected.

Even as she let Nganga go in peace, she carried the most intense, soul-stabbing pain I would witness later that day. Beneath her quiet grace, she was broken.

Two things can be true at once: she was loving and graceful, but the pain of losing her son would never truly heal. Grace and heartbreak lived side by side within her, defining the immeasurable love and loss of a mother.

A gentle push

A few weeks after I lost my brother, I began receiving FaceTime calls from Roger Grobler, one of the shareholders at Rain. Though he never said he was calling to check on me, I knew that's exactly what he was doing. Each call felt like a warm hug I hadn't known I needed.

I first met Roger outside the boardroom before presenting at my first Rain board meeting. His kind, calm demeanour struck me immediately. There was no air of self-importance about him, no sense of needing to prove anything. In the boardroom, he was clear, thoughtful, and deliberate, always sharing his ideas in a way that made you feel heard. I didn't realise then how much of an impact he'd have on me in the months after Nganga had left a heart-sized hole in my soul.

A few weeks after that first meeting, I flew from Johannesburg to Cape Town and happened to sit next to Roger on the flight. We both put our devices down and began to chat.

At some point, the conversation turned to church. He learned that I had spent my twenties as a devout Christian, leading cell groups and Bible studies. I'd even dabbled in Sunday School for a while. (I quickly discovered that Sunday School teaching was not my calling.) Roger told me about his time living in Australia and later India, where he and his wife had worked on projects to restore communities devastated by sexual violence. I no longer just saw him as a man in the boardroom, but as a human being who genuinely had a bleeding heart to help people.

Not long after that flight, Roger introduced me to Phil Dooley, the leader of Hillsong South Africa.

When I met Phil, I was surprised. He looked more like a surfer than a pastor. With his long, curly blond hair, tall frame, and perpetually sunny smile, he could have easily been mistaken for a hippy who cared more about waves than souls. But Phil's kindness was as apparent as his smile. He exuded a gentle warmth that immediately put me at ease.

Roger and Phil wanted my help developing a credo for the church. It was a tall ask because I had never done anything of the sort. They didn't want it to focus on theology but on the organisational principles that guided the church's leadership. The word *credo* means 'a statement of the beliefs or aims which guide someone's actions', and this was precisely what they wanted to create. They felt I could bring valuable insights to the process.

I hesitated at first. 'I don't go to church anymore,' I told Roger. 'He's not going to try to get me to go back, is he?'

Roger assured me Phil wasn't like that. He was right. When I met them both to work on the project, Phil didn't try any sly tactics that some pastors resort to when they are trying to grow a church. Phil knew that if you made people feel comfortable, they would want to join your church.

Not long after that meeting, my brother passed away.

I received a call from Brandon Leigh, the CEO of Rain, and it was more than just a call from a boss – it was from a human being who had been alongside me in the journey of trying to get my brother the help he needed.

I held my phone, watching 'Typing' linger on my screen. He was writing a long message because I'd been waiting for it for a long time. Then, instead of a message, the phone buzzed with an incoming WhatsApp call.

When I answered, his voice was raw, unsteady, burdened with an immense pain that I did not expect.

Until that moment, I had been operating in action mode – numb and mechanical, trying to navigate what had just happened. But as Brandon's words trembled through the phone, my throat constricted. Tears started forming, resting on the ledges of my eyelids beginning to trickle down my eyelashes. For the first time, I stepped out of action mode and was a brother who had lost a brother.

Roger must have heard about it from Brandon, because he also called me soon after I sent him a WhatsApp about Nganga's passing. He was not the only Rain board member to call. Many of the board members reached out to me – including Paul Harris (chairman of Rain and co-founder of FirstRand, one of the best businessmen in South Africa), Willem Roos (co-founder of OUTsurance), and Michael Jordaan, who spearheaded the impressive growth and innovation of First National Bank (FNB) during his tenure as CEO.

My first interaction with Michael Jordaan had been some years earlier, under very different circumstances. Frustrated with my bank at the time, I had vented on social media about my poor experience. To my surprise, a whole CEO of a major South African bank sent me a direct message on Twitter suggesting it might be time to switch. I stalled a bit, telling him that I had a few issues to sort out with my current bank and would switch in a few months. A few months later, while he was on holiday in Mauritius, he sent me another DM, asking when I was finally making the move to FNB. I was flummoxed. How could the CEO of a bank, someone I didn't know personally and who certainly had no reason to care about me – I wasn't even a high-net-worth client – be so invested in this? After I committed, he connected me with one of FNB's divisional heads, and I made the switch. That memory stayed with me, a testament to his hands-on approach and genuine investment in people.

Another board member who reached out was Ravi Naidoo, the visionary founder of Design Indaba, the world's largest design conference. My relationship with Ravi began years ago when I was a junior copywriter at The Jupiter Drawing Room in Cape Town. One day, senior leadership invited me to a meeting where they said that they had decided to resign the Design Indaba account, believing it wasn't worth the fees being charged.

Later that afternoon, I was unexpectedly called into the boardroom for a meeting. It was an unexpected set-up. Ravi sat alone on one side of the table, facing four senior agency members, as well my art director, Jamie Mietz, a senior and quiet but brilliant creative, and me, the junior.

Ravi walked into the boardroom like a supernova. I remember thinking, *Who is this Indian man walking in with such confidence?* He radiated an infectious energy, commanding the room with a positivity that felt larger than life. With his jacket off and his passion on full display, he spoke about his belief in South Africa. His words weren't just statements – they were a call to action. He painted a passionate vision of design as a vital tool for solving problems, driving innovation, and economic growth.

He spoke with the conviction of an evangelist. By the time he was done, the whole room was converted. Not a single person mentioned a word about resigning the account. Instead, they were talking about how we would go about making his vision come to life. For me, it was groundbreaking. Ravi was the first person of colour I had ever seen command a boardroom.

After that, I was invited to work on the Design Indaba campaign with Jamie Mietz. Together, we poured everything into the campaign. Our work paid off when the campaign won a Gold Eagle Award, one of the most prestigious honours in South African advertising. On the night of the awards, the stakes were raised even higher when the Black Eagle – an award so rare it hadn't been given in over a decade – was announced. To our astonishment, our campaign was the winner. It was an extraordinary moment, one Ravi celebrated with immense pride.

Over the years, Ravi and I stayed connected. When the telecom start-up Rain was searching for a Chief Marketing Officer, he put my name forward to the board and founders, believing in my potential. 'I've mentioned your name,' he told me, 'but the rest is up to you.' That confidence meant the world to me.

The other member of the board who contacted me to offer her condolences was Nicola Harris, founder of The Click Foundation. A former high-powered banker, she had shifted her focus to addressing literacy and numeracy challenges in underserved communities. In 2023, I accompanied Nicola to Mdantsane for the launch of the foundation's Eastern Cape initiative. The programme, which leverages technology to support both learners and teachers, was already showing remarkable results. In schools where it had been implemented, student performance in reading and maths had improved by over 40%.

Each call I received during those dark days reminded me of connections, of shared histories, and of the humanity that binds us all – even in our most isolated moments. But Roger's calls were different. They didn't just remind me of connection – they kept me tethered to it. He wouldn't leave me alone and let me retreat into isolation and self-pity during those dark days following Nganga's death. Roger's FaceTime calls kept coming.

Phil also reached out, offering his support. When I asked if I could use one of the Hillsong halls for Nganga's memorial service, he was more than happy to offer the space, as well as sound equipment and streaming services. His generosity allowed us to honour my brother in a way I will always be grateful for.

Months after Covid restrictions eased, Roger, Phil, and I resumed work on the credo, and we were able to finalise something the leadership team was happy with.

It was during one of those FaceTime calls that Roger broached the topic of therapy.

'Have you considered it?' he asked.

I hesitantly said that I had thought about it.

I think he could tell that thinking about it was all I was planning to do because his tone became concerned and firm – still kind, but unmistakably insistent. He urged me to give it a try, even if just for a single session. 'You might think you're fine,' he said, 'but you could be wrong. What's the harm in just seeing someone?'

I gave a lukewarm agreement and I thought that would be the end of it. I didn't think that therapy would come up again. Maybe Roger wouldn't even call back again. But he did. In fact, Roger called at least once a week, without fail. Each time, he asked about therapy. Not once did he bring up work, which surprised me. Here was a high-powered corporate board member, someone who surely had a packed schedule, yet he cared enough to follow up with me consistently.

By the third or fourth call (maybe the fifth – I can't be sure), Roger's persistence reached a new level. This time, he came armed with a shortlist of therapists near me, even mentioning one in Claremont. His determination, and the fact that he even took the trouble to find therapists around De Waterkant, where I lived, so that I wouldn't have too far to go, finally hit me. I realised that I couldn't keep brushing it off. So, I started asking around, reaching out to friends to see if they could recommend someone. Roger's insistence had moved me from avoidance to action.

A friend, Iman Mkwanazi, suggested a young therapist she thought highly of, but I was slightly reluctant. She was too young, I thought. After what seemed like a Tinder selection process for a therapist, I eventually decided on the therapist Roger had found in Claremont. He was older, a professor, someone I felt had the life experience and gravitas I needed.

At a time when I might have accepted the easy temptation of pulling away from the world, Roger's quiet persistence pulled me closer. He didn't demand or impose, but instead, became the steady presence I didn't know I needed. He didn't drag me into therapy, but he also didn't allow me to retreat into the shadows. Years earlier, Trevor Noah had booked that doctor's appointment when I wouldn't. Now Roger was doing the same – seeing me when I couldn't see myself clearly, refusing to let me get lost in the weight of my grief.

Life is like that sometimes

What they both taught me wasn't just about therapy or doctor's appointments. It was about what it means to truly see someone. To show up. To hold a mirror when they've lost sight of themselves, proving that help isn't a burden to be hidden, but a weight that becomes bearable when carried together.

The professor therapist

One of the small joys of selecting a therapist all the way in Claremont was the drive. Leaving my apartment in De Waterkant, where my brother's absence brushed against me constantly, felt freeing. The streets were Covidly empty, and I could enjoy the purr of the Jaguar as it hugged the twisting turns of Hospital Bend, past UCT and into Newlands. Those drives gave me space to clear my head before confronting what waited for me at the therapist's home office.

When I first arrived at this therapist's home, there was no sense of embarrassment this time, no reception desk, no clinic signage. I put on my mask and rang the bell at the gate. It buzzed open and an elderly man in his seventies, masked but smiling beneath it, greeted me warmly.

He asked if it would be okay for him to remove his mask, assuring me that he would maintain a safe distance. He added that I could remove mine too, if I felt comfortable. We both did, keeping a safe distance apart.

We began with small talk. He asked what had brought me there and what I hoped to achieve.

'Grief counselling,' I said.

He nodded. 'What happened?'

And so I began to tell him. I kept the story simple, factual, avoiding emotion. I told him about my brother.

My brother lived with me.

I loved him.

He loved me.

I brought him to Cape Town from Mdantsane near East London for a job.

He worked with me.

I saw him every day.

He was the youngest in the family.

I have two sisters and a mother.

My father died when I was five, just before I turned six.

Then the harder parts:

I came back from holiday to find household items missing.

He did not tell the truth about what had happened.

I eventually got him to confess.

He had a gambling problem, he said.

I thought we could fix it. I told him it was fine, that we would work through it. He was relieved. I was relieved. For a while, it seemed we were getting better. Then he got worse.

I had to fire him.

I forced him to tell our mother.

Again, he seemed to recover. I found him a therapist. I thought we were making progress. He was telling me he was getting better.

Then he got worse again.

I kicked him out of my place.

I left for the weekend for Johannesburg on Thursday.

On Friday afternoon, I got a phone call that he had taken his life.

For 20 or 30 minutes, I recounted the story. The professor sat listening attentively, saying nothing. When I finished, he reached for a clipboard and began asking me questions. With each answer, he marked a mysterious box. The questions went on for what seemed like half an hour.

Finally, he said, 'When you first told me the story, I thought I would need to prescribe anti-depressants. But based on your answers to my questions, you don't need them. That's good news. But remember, there's nothing wrong with medication – it serves a very good purpose for those who need it.'

I was relieved to hear that, though I couldn't quite say why.

• • •

In the next session, we spoke more about my family background.

My grandparents, who raised me until I was ten.

My mother and siblings.

What it meant being the first-born and the responsibilities that came with it.

When we eventually came to my brother, I shared something I hadn't told anyone.

'After I kicked him out for that weekend, my plan when I returned from Johannesburg was to send him back to the Eastern Cape to re-evaluate his life. Not to my mother in Mdantsane, but to Dutyini, the village where I was born. I thought the boredom of the village would do him good. My mother had sent him there for about six months a few years before, and when he came back, he'd lost weight – not out of frustration, but because he'd started running and working out with our cousins. He had missed city life, but he'd been happy there.'

I hesitated. 'But I never shared that plan with him. Maybe if I had told him that I was going to send him to the village, he might not have taken the drastic steps he took. I still feel guilty about it. Maybe I want to believe that would have changed the outcome. I don't know.'

The professor listened, then said, 'I can see it's quite difficult for you, the suicide. Suicide is difficult. And it's not something we're often able to speak about openly. There's a pressure to suppress the feelings, to hold it all together, because there's no outlet for that kind of pain.'

He was right about suppressing it. I didn't want pity, even well-meaning pity. I wanted people to see me as fine. I wanted them to know that what happened to my brother wouldn't happen to me. So I made the jokes first. I squashed the awkward silences, never allowing time for a pity party.

'Even when I'm not fine, I'm still fine,' I told him, echoing a line from the TV show, *The Good Wife*. That's what I needed people to believe.

•••

The professor was good. He asked the right questions, he challenged and redirected my thinking, and pushed me to confront things I hadn't wanted to face.

But he lost me the day he began to make assumptions.

'There's still that "I don't have a father" thing,' he said. 'You don't have anyone you could model yourself on as a father figure.' He had forgotten what I had told him before.

I corrected him politely. 'I had my grandfather. I spent every day with him. He was a role model I looked up to, along with the whole community. I also had uncles in my life.'

It wasn't just what he said that felt like a slap in the face – it was what they represented. It felt like a familiar and lazy narrative, a default assumption about young black men that lacked any sense of nuance. It was frustrating, not because it was directed at me specifically, but because it was so broad and thoughtless. I felt as though he had reduced my experience to a copy-and-paste template. *Am I not worth listening to? This is exactly why I should have gone to see a black therapist like I had the first time around,* I thought to myself.

He made several other assumptions after that and almost undid the good work he had done. I corrected him politely again.

To his credit, right at the beginning of our next session, he apologised. 'I made assumptions last week, and I got a few things terribly wrong,' he said.

It was not something I had expected. In fact, I had already decided that session would be my last. I walked in convinced it would confirm what I had begun to suspect: that he was misguided about black people and that I was wasting my time.

When he began with his apology, I felt both impressed and relieved. If I'm honest, I had expected him to be no different from the many elderly white people I've encountered who hold tightly to their misplaced views about black people, no matter how biased or uninformed.

During our previous session, when I corrected him, he had neither paused nor acknowledged what I had said. He had simply moved on, as if I hadn't spoken, and that had left me deeply disappointed. *I am spending so much money on these sessions, and this is what I am getting?* I thought.

I had assumed my corrections had gone unnoticed, or worse, ignored entirely. But here he was, starting the session with a sincere apology. It caught me off guard, disarmed me in a way I hadn't expected. For the first time, I felt like he had seen me – not through the lens of his assumptions, but as I was. That mattered more than I realised in that moment. It was enough to make me stay.

Guilt and grief

Whether therapy freed me from the feelings of guilt I carried, I still cannot say. What I can say is that it helped me understand it. The guilt was not me. It did not define me. It was a heavy, intrusive, and unwelcome passenger, but not the sum of who I was. Still, it persisted, whispering doubts, replaying moments I couldn't change, weaving itself into the rhythm of my daily life.

Nganga's actions left me with a lingering burden of uncertainty, a quiet erosion of the confidence I once had in my decision-making. The certainty I relied on was stripped away, leaving every choice feeling like a potential landmine. *What if this is the wrong decision? What if everything falls apart because of it?* These questions were constant companions, turning even the smallest choices into burdens.

The guilt was stubborn, lurking in the back of my thoughts, setting up camp as a clanging cymbal in the quiet spaces of my mind. It manifested as self-doubt, as an unwillingness to trust my instincts.

I didn't realise it at the time, but my work began to suffer. People around me relied on my clarity, on my ability to make decisions with conviction and with speed. Haste was needed because I worked for a fast-growing start-up – there was no time for snails. But my conviction had ebbed away, replaced by second-guessing myself constantly and a fear of making decisions.

I knew, intellectually, that Nganga's suicide was his choice. It was his hand that had ended his life. I understood that as fact. But my feelings hadn't caught up to my mind.

Therapy did not completely erase the guilt, but it did something almost as important: it gave it shape. It gave it edges, boundaries, a name. I learned to see it as something I carried, not something that defined me. It was a feeling, not an identity. Therapy helped me grab back a sense of control over the guilt, to take back the space it had tried to claim.

It didn't vanish, but it became manageable. Something I could hold at arm's length and understand, even if I couldn't yet let it go.

· · ·

While therapy gave me tools to understand my own guilt, it couldn't touch the silence that surrounded us as a family. Perhaps the most difficult part of grieving is the silence. The way it hangs in the room, heavy and unyielding, as if waiting for someone brave enough to acknowledge it. My family and I spoke, of course, but never about Nganga. Never about the weight of his absence, what it meant, how we were dealing with it. The loss hung over all of us, too big and too painful to name or give a label to what we were feeling. Avoiding it all together felt better than touching the wound. We were grieving, but we were each grieving alone – together.

My sisters and mother were in the Eastern Cape together. I was far away from them, in Cape Town. I imagined that they carried the grief and saw it in each other's eyes daily but avoided talking about it because none of them wanted to make the wound bigger. I called my mother on FaceTime constantly because I feared how badly she was taking the loss. She was his mother. She had buried a son. Her last born.

But I never asked her about her grief. I never spoke of mine. Maybe we were trying to build a fragile truce around the edges of our sorrow, pretending the sadness wasn't there. But it was, as constant and unyielding as waves during a storm, smashing into a rocky coastline.

I am going to die next year

'Ndizakufa kunyaka ozayo.' ('I am going to die next year.')

These were the words my mother said when we were finally alone with my sisters, Siki and Siku, after Nganga's funeral service.

The cousins, relatives, and friends had left. Silence sat with us, a relentless and uninvited guest. The house, once crowded with noise, was too quiet now. The TV was on, but no one was watching. Our eyes darted everywhere but towards each other. None of us wanted to break again – we were broken enough.

Her words escaped her lips weakly, almost as if they were meant only for herself. But the house was too silent not to hear them. The weight of her statement settled into the room, heavier than anything I'd felt that day.

Fear and disbelief churned in me, volcanic and unstoppable. *We can't lose her now. We've already lost too much to endure another loss. There is no way we could survive losing her too.*

Her gaze was fixed on the floor, but it seemed as though she was staring at something far beyond it – an invisible horizon only she could see. Perhaps she was looking at Nganga, walking into the sunset. Or maybe she was looking into her own sunset.

It seemed to me my mother had resigned herself and was in a special hurry. I could not accept that. I had never seen her this way before, as if she had already decided. The thought of her willing this fate into existence sent me into action.

'Ungayithethi lento uyithethatyo. Uyitsholo ntoni lento? Ukukho nto njalo ezakwenzeka.' ('Don't say this thing you are saying. What are you saying it for? No such thing is going to happen.')

But she responded as if she hadn't heard me. 'My mother also died the following year after Sbongile died.'

Bhut' Sbongile was her younger brother. And it is true that my grandmother passed on the year after my uncle, her son, died in a tragic accident. This wasn't just grief – it was as if she was telling Makhulu, 'Now I finally understand what you were going through. Now it is my turn.'

For the first time, I fully understood the saying that no parent should ever have to bury their child. I could see the inexpressible anguish all over her face. Nganga was her last-born child, and like so many parents, she had always reserved a special softness for him.

I had been surprised by how graciously she had handled what Nganga had done. She was heartbroken, but there was no anger. Somehow, she understood his choice. Even in her pain, she found a grace that caught me off guard.

But I couldn't accept what she was saying now. I would not. She still had three other children. Her death wasn't an option. She was a strong woman. She was too strong to succumb to this.

I had seen how strong she was in the days leading up to the funeral. She had flown to Cape Town for Nganga's memorial service with my sisters, cousins, and aunt. I had been quietly surprised and encouraged by how well she was carrying the loss. She still joked and smiled, and her calm had given me a fragile sense of hope, even as I judged myself harshly for what had happened to Nganga.

Perhaps she knew me better than I thought and the act she put on was for me, knowing I already carried enough guilt. Her strength and her mother's love were the armour I didn't know I needed. I did not know then that her stoicism for those two days in Cape Town, before she flew back to continue mourning in Mdantsane, was a gift she was giving me.

When she said she was going to die next year, my mind flashed back to the crematorium after Nganga's service. She had walked out ahead of me, and I followed her. Suddenly, she stopped and leaned against the hearse, pressing her forehead against her hands on the window. She didn't fall, but she collapsed into herself.

For the first time, I saw her cry. Her body began to heave with shallow breaths as grief overtook her. It was just the two of us. I put my arms around her, rubbing her back, not knowing what to say. What can a grieving son say to a grieving mother who has had to bury a last-born child?

People began to pour out of the chapel, and I asked her to sit in the car. I did not wish for her to get well-meaning, pitiful glances from people. She was a proud woman and she would have hated to be seen like that, even though it was the right time to be vulnerable.

Later, as I drove home, my mind replayed the moment I first heard Nganga was gone. I had told Siki not to let our mother speak to me after she found out. I did not want to hear the crack in her voice. Nganga was in my care, and we lost him in my care. I was not there when he died. I was cold to him. I had rejected him. My heart was heavy.

Barely an hour after she got the news of my brother's passing, my mother called me from my sister's phone. I didn't know what to say to her. I was deeply sad.

Her voice was calm. 'Uyazazi uba uzofika nini?' ('Do you know when you will be coming down?')

I told her my plan: fly to Cape Town the next morning, identify Nganga's body, arrange his transport to East London, and hold a memorial service in Cape Town so the people there could say their goodbyes. She listened.

Her calm acceptance in that moment felt incomprehensible. But now, I think she was protecting me in the only way she could. Even in her devastation, she was still my mother first.

She's been hospitalised

'Ndizakufa kunyaka ozayo.' ('I am going to die next year.') Those words, spoken by my mother after Nganga's funeral, tortured me for a long time. In fact, they never stopped haunting me in the years that followed. I couldn't accept them. I refused to. Denial was easier than confronting the cruel weight of what felt like a prophecy. I buried those words in the chaos of life, hoping they would stay there, dismissed as grief's careless whisper. But as time passed, they began to feel less like grief and more like a truth biding its time, slowly revealing itself as my mother started to fade.

She didn't die the next year, but grief has a way of stealing pieces of you long before the final act. Time etched its toll into her face, her voice, her spirit. By the time January 2024 arrived, it seemed her soul had been quietly preparing for what her body was finally succumbing to.

There are phone calls that feel like the first pull of an unstoppable thread, the kind that slowly undoes everything you've managed to hold together. That's what it felt like when my sister called to tell me that our mother had been hospitalised. Earlier that day, they'd taken her to the doctor, and it hadn't sounded like it was a big deal. She often went for medication or check-ups, so I hadn't given it much thought. But now, Siki was telling me she'd been admitted for observation, and I couldn't make sense of it.

I was driving in Bryanston, Gauteng, on my way to visit my friend, Karabo Songo. It was early evening in December, that time of year when South Africans discard their troubles, ready to pick them up again in January. I was in a good mood. Karabo and I, along with a big team, had just delivered a highly praised advertising campaign promoting international tourism to South Africa, featuring Trevor Noah. The Springboks had recently won the 2023 Rugby World Cup, becoming the second back-to-back winners of the title, and the only team to have captured the cup four times. South Africa was in high spirits. Yet beneath it all, real life was happening.

The phone call from my sister was a slap back to reality that nobody expects during a South African December.

Her tone was calm – too calm – and I didn't take it well. 'There is no need to panic,' she said.

'The doctor recommended that they observe her in hospital for a few days,' she reassured me. But why would a doctor suggest hospitalisation out of the blue if it wasn't serious? My mind raced. How bad was she, really? I wanted to know.

There was a disconnect between the conversation I'd had with my mother on the phone the day before – when there was no mention of any unusual ill health – and this sudden hospitalisation that troubled me deeply. I directed my anxiety at the people on the other end of the line. If anyone had been in the car with me, they might have mistaken me for a corporate executive grilling his juniors after a project had gone catastrophically wrong. I demanded details. Timelines. I was certainly not a good brother in that moment.

'But you guys were just at the doctor yesterday. I thought he was just checking her and giving her meds. What changed?'

When Siki couldn't satisfy my need for details and realised that I was treating her like a direct report at work, she passed the phone to our older cousin, Sis' Nobulali Mshumi, who tried to placate me. I was convinced they were stage-managing the situation to keep me from worrying, so her reassurances only increased my anxiety. I sent follow-up texts, asking how my mother was and what the doctor had said. Again, they told me not to panic. I tried. Unsuccessfully.

I soon got another call from my aunt who was less than pleased with me for upsetting everyone else with my interrogation. I asked if I needed to leave Johannesburg and come to East London, and she said not yet, that everything was under control, that I was already coming down in a few days for the December holidays so there was no need to hurry, that they just needed to get tests done in hospital.

When I arrived at Karabo's house, I sat in the car for a while, trying to process and gather my thoughts. I shared with Karabo that my mother had been hospitalised, downplaying how I was feeling. It was the same story I repeated to others – minimising my own fear, trying to convince myself it wasn't that serious. It could not be that serious because I did not want it to be. I willed it not to be. I tried to 'god' it into being something minor, as if my thoughts and my will were the strongest forces in the universe. I prayed desperately as though sheer determination and faith could bend reality to my desire.

• • •

The days passed, and my mother remained in hospital. I was relieved to hear that Sis' Thozeka, my dad's sister, who was also a nurse, was seeing her every day, along with Siki and Siku. But the fact that she was still a patient in that bed gnawed at me. It didn't feel like a 'routine check' anymore.

When I finally arrived in the Eastern Cape, after an eight-hour drive from Johannesburg, the first stop I made was the hospital. My mother had been there for almost a week.

As I entered the ward, my nervousness grew. I didn't know if it was guilt or fear – or both – but whatever it was, I did not feel comfortable. The wide hospital corridors seemed to stretch endlessly. Then, chaos erupted.

A commotion broke out in a nearby corridor – shouting, running, the sound of what I can only describe as a stampede of fat sheep. A few security guards ran past me. A family sitting on a nearby bench along the wall, in direct sight of what was going on, stood up and scattered in all directions, leaving behind a small boy who began screaming.

Seeing that everyone had left him, I ran towards him and grabbed him. He gripped on to me, a complete stranger, so tightly that it felt like his life depended on me in that moment. Around the corner, there was a big, topless, coloured young man in his mid-twenties being pursued by five or six security guards and three other people, who I assumed were family members. Some were on the ground – he'd clearly pushed them out of the way.

The little boy in my arms had his mouth open wide as he was pulling in as much air into his lungs as he possibly could – long enough for a 100-metre Olympian to finish a race. He then belted out a scream that echoed through the hospital wing. The security guards pursuing the man finally pinned him to the ground until he had little strength left to fend them off. As the wrestling match began to die down, the boy's family emerged sheepishly and took him from my arms. The coloured man was dragged back to the ward.

The absurdity of the moment jarred me, and yet it provided a momentary distraction from the weight of what I was about to face. I thought about how my mother would have found the scene thoroughly entertaining, how she would have made a meal of retelling this story if she had been the one to witness it.

When I reached my mother's ward, she was lying on her side, facing the window. She seemed to be sleeping. 'Anti,' I said softly as I approached her.

Her eyes fluttered open, and for a moment, I felt the loss I was trying so hard to ignore. Her face was thinner than I'd ever seen it, her features gaunt and haunted by a ghost that seemed determined to take her. I saw little fight in her – and I had always known her to fight.

She gave me the faintest smile, one that seemed to drain all the energy from her, and then closed her eyes again.

Maybe it's because she is drugged, I told myself, denying the presence I felt of the ghost that seemed to hover, waiting.

I sat quietly, unsure what to say or do. She was clearly exhausted. I called for a doctor to give me details.

They said the drugs were making her look this way. They did not know what was wrong. They were conducting a series of tests, they said. She was on strong pain medication. There was a growth in her ovary, but they wouldn't know more until they had the results.

They had drilled into her spinal cord for a bone marrow biopsy because they wanted to know if it was bone marrow cancer. I asked if that was a good idea, given her weakened state.

Looking through the doctor's notes, I noticed a glaring omission. 'Why doesn't this mention that she had cervical cancer in 2011?' I asked. 'She went through radiation and was declared cancer-free.'

'She had cervical cancer? She did not mention that,' the doctor said.

I shook my head knowingly. Of course, she hadn't mentioned it. My mother was stubborn and proud to a fault. She had probably decided it was not worth bringing up.

Later, when I told her that I had let the doctors know about her history of cancer, she was upset with me, her tone laced with disapproval. 'They didn't need to know that. Why would you do that?' she said, as though it were a minor detail, as though it had no bearing on her current condition.

I tried to reason with her. 'They need the full picture to treat you properly,' I said. But in that moment, I could tell she had already decided what mattered and what didn't, what she would share and what she would carry silently.

I think she's given up, I told myself. The thought punched me, but I wasn't ready to accept it. No. I wouldn't let her give up. I couldn't. If she had resigned, I would fight for her.

That was not the first time her pride had kept me in the dark. When she was first diagnosed with cervical cancer in 2011, she hid it from everyone. It wasn't until she had been undergoing radiation treatments once a week for over a month – enduring it quietly, alone – that she finally told me.

I was furious. I closed the door to my office, paced up and down the small space and did what parents do to their children when they find out they've been keeping secrets: I scolded her.

'Why didn't you tell me sooner? Why did you go through this alone?' I had demanded, my worry spilling out as anger.

Her response had been as typical as it was maddening. I could picture the shrug, and the dismissive wave of her hand from her tone on the phone call, as if to say, 'I handled it, didn't I?'

That was my mother – unyielding in her independence, determined to carry her burdens alone. Even now, when she needed help the most, she couldn't bear to let anyone truly see the weight she was carrying – even if she had given up. She would not want anyone to see that she had given up.

The doctor assured me she was in good hands and that I should come back the next day, that my mother would look better once the medication wore off. I wanted to believe it, but a part of me was convinced these were my mother's last days.

The next day, she was sitting up in bed but still in great pain. I had brought her the food she had asked me for. Earlier that day, a colleague had called me, followed by a stream of emails about a PowerPoint presentation that, apparently, couldn't wait. And I'd looked at it. I'd opened my laptop, reviewed the slides, made edits, given input – immersing myself in the triviality of bullet points and meaningless lines of copy while my mother lay in a hospital bed, teetering between life and death.

Why? Why did I do that? Maybe I paid attention to the presentation because it was easier than facing the reality of her fragility. But even as I clicked through those slides, a voice in my head screamed, *What the hell is wrong with you?* I justified it by telling myself that everyone else was looking to me to do it.

If I could go back, I'd ignore the emails, the calls, the Teams meetings I answered when I should have been with my mother. None of it mattered. The only thing that mattered was her. If there's any regret that gnaws at me now, it's the time I spent on that PowerPoint presentation instead of being fully present with her – holding her hand, telling her how much I loved her in a moment when every second mattered more than I realised.

She did improve and looked much better over the next few days – still in pain, but more like herself. Each day I visited after that, she seemed to be improving but remained weak and bedridden. She was still the feisty, sometimes irritating woman I'd always known. That gave me hope, but it was a fragile hope.

'I would rather she be alive, well, healthy, and irritating than how she is now, Lord,' I whispered in prayer.

Out in the cold

It was a normal, uneventful, and perfectly forgettable Monday. Johannesburg's January summer heat was relentless, pressing into everything. I was in the small Until Until offices on the first floor of Parktown Quarter, where our team shared space with Uber's multi-billion-dollar operation. Below us were a Woolworths, a liquor store, an optometrist, and a Kauai where I ordered the same thing every day for lunch.

I had just returned from buying a bottle of sparkling water at Woolworths when I leaned my sizeable Xhosa man gluteus maximus on the corner of a desk. Without warning, the desk began to descend in slow motion.

As I felt the desk collapse beneath me, I realised what was happening but couldn't really believe it. Moments later, I had to resign myself to the inevitable collapse of the desk, trying to minimise the impact by jumping off it before I crashed onto the floor, along with the furniture.

Hearing the commotion, Amahle Jaxa stepped out of the boardroom with her hand over her mouth. 'Are you okay?' she asked.

I was on the floor. Amahle was concerned but I started

laughing. A loud belly laugh came out of me as I picked myself up from the now collapsed desk. I probably looked like the human embodiment of a ROFL emoji – sprawled out, laughing uncontrollably, surrounded by the ruins of the desk. Once everyone in the office saw I was fine, they joined in the laugher.

It wasn't entirely my fault – the desk was old and poorly constructed, and it had looked deceptively sturdy. Lenzo Mangonyane and Gaba Guliwe helped me pick up the broken pieces, laughing as we carried them to a backroom storeroom. There, we found a wobbly replacement desk. It inspired no confidence itself but was just stable enough to survive for the day.

As I sat back down, I glanced at my phone and saw two missed calls from my aunt, Thozeka Mancotywa (my late father's sister), and WhatsApp messages from my sister, Siki. The date on my phone read 22 January. I had planned to visit my mother in Mdantsane on 25 January.

My aunt and Siki, who were in East London, had been keeping me updated regularly on my mother's condition since I had returned to Johannesburg. Just a few days earlier, the news had been encouraging: she was improving, sitting up in her hospital bed without much assistance, and Siku had even mentioned arranging physiotherapy to help her stand and walk again. For the first time in weeks, I'd begun to feel cautiously optimistic when their calls came through.

But that Monday, the notifications were clustered together – two missed calls and back-to-back messages. The first read: 'Sis' Thozeka is trying to call', followed by: 'It's important' with a praying emoji. The urgency in her tone was unmistakable. I could see the missed call notification from my aunt: 13:12. Siki's messages were sent at 13:13, just moments apart. My reply, promising to call back, was logged at 13:16.

I walked into an empty meeting room to return the call.

'Molo, sisi,' I said.

'Molo. Ayikho mnandi le nto ndizakukuxelela yona.' ('Hi. What I am about to say to you is not nice.')

I knew immediately. I was just waiting for her to land the blow – like a boxer who could see their opponent's fist swinging but knew there was no time to duck.

'Usisi usishiyile. Ngxesi khehle.' ('Sisi has left us. I am so sorry.')

'Okay, sisi.' I said.

'Ngxesi khehle,' she said again.

'Okay, sisi. Enkosi.' I thanked her.

'Ngxesi Diba.' ('I am sorry, Diba.')

'Enkosi, sisi. Kulungile.' ('Thank you, sisi. It's fine.') I was not fine, but it was an automatic response, I suppose. Even when I am not fine, I am still fine.

Then there was silence. I didn't know if there was something I was supposed to say or do at the time. I was unnervingly calm, if not cold. Yes. Cold. It was a coldness that moved all over my body with nowhere to go. It is difficult to say what I felt in that moment – whatever it was, it was foreign. It was there and not there. There was emotion and no emotion. But I do remember the loneliness and coldness of it all.

The call ended. Exactly 59 seconds long. I stood there, motionless, trying to understand why I felt ... nothing. The room was empty. I was empty. Cold. Numb.

Why am I not crying? Why do I have no emotions? Did I not love my mother? Did I think I loved her but didn't? Was this guilt? Was I even a good son to her?

Pull yourself together, I told myself, thinking I should get back to work.

At my desk, shock set in. To my colleagues, I probably looked focused, even though I was unravelling inside. My mind returned to the last time I had seen her, lying in that hospital bed. I thought she was getting better.

I thought about those 'urgent' emails and PowerPoint presentation I had worked on while my mother lay there. I wondered if the dead could see the choices we made before they left us. Would she see me hunched over my laptop at the hospital, fine-tuning slides and adjusting bullet points when I should have been sitting beside her? Would she watch a reel of my misplaced priorities and wonder if I cared enough? In the end, maybe I was not a good son.

Sitting at that desk, trying to work, felt like an Oscar award-winning performance. But then I started to feel bouts of grief coming in, like a late-afternoon Johannesburg thunderstorm. I realised I did not want the storm to strike while I was in the office. I was beginning to feel the drops of emotion hitting slowly as the distant Johannesburg afternoon storm closed in.

I left the office in a hurry, fabricating an excuse about a meeting. Another Oscar award-winning performance on my part.

I got to my car and for the first time, felt so completely and utterly alone. I felt blackness and blankness. With my mother gone, I was untethered. No parents. No grandparents. I felt adrift in a cold, dark, black, lifeless ocean, without an anchor.

The woman who had carried me, shaped me, and stood strong even in her own pain was no longer here.

Where does it hurt, Mother?

It does not matter how old you are; when your mother tells you she's proud of you, it gives you a sense of invincibility – even when you feel you haven't done anything to deserve it. A hundred people could tell you you're worthless, but if your mother believes in you, their words fall away like dust.

Two years before my mother passed away, she told me she'd finally read my books, *To Quote Myself* and *These Things Really Do Happen To Me*.

'Ewe wethu ndidunyelwe yilencwadi uyibhale kamnandi kangaka ucacisa ndothuke nezinto ozaziyo kodwa wawumncinci. Ndikhunjuzwa yint'uba bayifunda kule ndawo yefuneral yhoo hai uyabhala bend'beva bantu bekuncoma ngekhe, uyayenza into yakho. Ibingafundwa naseskolweni kuba azaziwa ngabantu belixesha nabakhulele ezidolophini.' ('I am so impressed and proud of the books you wrote. You wrote it so beautifully and I was surprised by all the things you remember because you were young then. I am reminded by the part you wrote about the funeral. It could be read even in schools because there are many things that people who grew up in the cities do not know you wrote about.')

The story she mentioned – the one about the funeral – was about my father's burial. I was six years old, holding my mother's hand tightly as we stood by the gravesite. My father's coffin had just been lowered into the ground. Beside her, older women flanked her on either side, whispering words I couldn't hear, urging her forward. She was swaying slightly, her feet hesitating. Then, they pushed her towards the grave.

I didn't understand what was happening, but I thought the grown-ups were trying to push my mother into the hole with the coffin. I panicked. I grabbed her hand tighter and pulled with all my might, screaming to stop them. I wasn't letting them take her too.

It startled the people nearby. They must have thought I was crying for my father, but I wasn't. I was crying for her.

I think if they had pushed her in, I would have jumped in after her.

After reading this story in *To Quote Myself,* my mother told me, sadness fell upon her again because it allowed another memory to resurface. It wasn't the burial she remembered but the moment she realised how much I wanted to protect her.

After throwing dirt into the open grave, my grandmother – my mother's mother – and her great aunt flanked her as they walked her back to the car.

Our family graves are on an old family plot of land where the Dlangas had originally settled in Danti. There is no trace of the houses my grandfather, Thambile Paulos Dlanga, built many years ago. The plot sits on top of a hill in the village, enclosed by a fence.

It's just a short walk from the church. There is no road leading to the simple village church, so cars are left further down. Footpaths in the grass, carved by the steady steps of villagers walking to church over the years, are the only way up.

As they walked on the uneven grass of the footpath, my mother, newly widowed at 26 years old, was overwhelmed by the reality of loss. She had already felt like a single mother for some time, but losing my father that day made it final. She later told me she remembered the man he had been before Johannesburg, before he abandoned us. A kind and good man.

Her headscarf had slipped low over her eyebrows, obscuring her vision. She had not wanted to be seen crying in the church because, even then, she was a proud woman.

She stopped and kneeled on the grass, asking her mother and great aunt to fix the headwrap so that she could see properly. They gave her water to drink and wash her face – as if washing away the shadow of her grief.

That's when I arrived. When I saw her wet face, I unbuttoned my shirt, took her big hand into my own, and used the fabric to wipe her face.

'Uyagula, anti? Uzophila, anti. Kubuhlungu phi?' ('Are you sick, aunty? You will heal, aunty. Where does it hurt?')

As I look back now, I think that was the first time I'd tried to take her pain away. It wouldn't be the last.

She often told me how proud she was of me, but now I see how much of my own strength I've borrowed from her. Her resilience wasn't something she spoke about – it was something she lived.

When I wrote about that day at the funeral, she said it moved her. But what I think moved her most was remembering how deeply I'd always loved her – even when I was too young to understand what love, or heartbreak, really were.

Notes

1. Information sourced from *BusinessTech*, 14 August 2016, 'South Africa's skewed income distribution when measured by race', as accessed online at Businesstech.co.za.
2. Information sourced from *Mail & Guardian*, 10 January 2023, 'More black fiction writers need to be published in South Africa' by Thabo Miya, as accessed online at Mg.co.za.
3. Scripture taken from the New International Version® (NIV). Copyright © 1973, 1978, 1984, 2011 by Biblica, Inc.®, as accessed online at Bible.com.
4. This Bible verse is from *Izibhalo Ezingcwele* (The Holy Scriptures), Xhosa Bible, 1975 translation (XHO75). © Bible Society of South Africa, 1975, as accessed online at Bible.com.
5. Scripture taken from the New International Version® (NIV). Copyright © 1973, 1978, 1984, 2011 by Biblica, Inc.®, as accessed online at Bible.com.
6. Scripture taken from the New King James Version® (NKJV). Copyright © 1982 by Thomas Nelson, as accessed online at Bible.com.
7. Scripture taken from the New International Version® (NIV). Copyright © 1973, 1978, 1984, 2011 by Biblica, Inc.®, as accessed online at Bible.com.
8. Quote from *Long Walk to Freedom* by Nelson Mandela, chapter 70. Copyright © 1994 by Nelson Rolihlahla Mandela. Published by Little, Brown and Company, 1994. Reproduced with permission of the Licensor through PLSclear.

Acknowledgements

Writing a book may feel like a solitary act – just a writer facing the blinking cursor – but it is never truly done alone. So many people, knowingly or unknowingly, contributed to the words on these pages, even if their names never appear within them.

To my remaining immediate family, **Sikelelwa** and **Sikulo Dlanga**, thank you for helping me remember the stories of our childhood. I know that reading this book will not be easy for you, as you have lived through the same losses and endured so much. You cared for our mother with a love and devotion that words cannot fully capture, especially during her final days when I could not be there, bound by my life in Johannesburg.

To my aunt, **Nolulama Mshumi**, who shared some kind words after I lost my dear brother Nganga, and her daughter, **Nobulali Mshumi**, who sat at my mother's hospital bedside daily, along with my aunts **Thozeka Mancotya** and **Ondisa Dlanga** – your care and presence gave her strength in her final moments.

To my friends who supported me through some of the hardest days of my life, thank you for your kindness, patience, and unwavering presence. **Xolisa Dyeshana**, my cousin and my anchor. **Anele Mdoda**, who hilariously called me two days before my mother's funeral, saying, 'Chap, I must make a confession. I used your mother's passing as an excuse to avoid going to a lunch I didn't want to go to. I said I had to go buy things for your sisters for your mother's funeral – what they want is only available in Johannesburg and your sisters are in East London.' It was brilliant because I could see myself doing the same thing. **Trevor Noah** and **Sizwe Dhlomo** – you each lifted me up when I needed it most. Trevor, your long phone calls from across the ocean reminded me that no distance can diminish true friendship.

To my colleagues from Heineken, **Themba Ratsibe** and **Dimakatso Napiane**, thank you for going beyond the call of duty. **Sthe Mabanga** and **Sanele Zondi**, your unexpected support during my time of need was deeply moving.

To **Minenhle Dlamini**, who called me a few weeks after we buried Nganga. For the first time when she called, I felt that there was someone who truly understood and grasped what I was going through. She too had lost her own brother just five months before. Thank you for your support and for making me feel understood.

To friends like **Karabo Songo, Molebogeng Mogotsi, Ayanda Thabethe**, whose support went beyond anything I imagined, I am eternally grateful. To **Lesedi Phala, Wendy Palaza, Zamokuhle Vilakazi, Nompumelelo Sithole, Musa Mzoneli, Tshepo Phakathi, Zezimdumise Nxumalo, Gcinikhaya Gobodo, Litha Nkombisa, Ciko Thomas, Vusani Malie, Romeo Khumalo, Athi Geleba** and **Khethang Malefane**, who travelled from Johannesburg to East London with a broken back – standing the entire flight to and from – your sacrifice humbles me.

To **Simphiwe Nghona, Nhlanhla Mbele, Siyasa Khashe,**

the **Macozoma family**, and the **Mgugudo family** – thank you for your enduring care and encouragement.

To **Neo Nontso** and **Mkhululi Mabhena**, who, upon hearing of my mother's passing, immediately sprang into action, baking scones and bringing them to me before I flew to East London to be with my sisters – thank you for your kindness.

To **Noni Gasa** and **Sindiswa Ndlovu**, who refused to let me take an Uber from the airport, and to **Shaka Sisulu**, who would not let me drive myself to the airport – thank you for being there.

To **Moshe Ndiki**, who dropped everything from his busy schedule and cancelled money-making events to MC his friend's, Nganga's, memorial service with grace and humour that carried us.

To **Kanyisa Limekaya**, who, himself, was going through the most heartbreaking grief, and still came through to support my family.

To my extended **Dlanga**, **Boyce**, **Dandala** clans for being there and **Professor Somadoda Fikeni**. Your presence and unwavering support mean more to me than words can express.

To **Thobeka Dandala**, who has become my unofficial family confidant from the days we worked at Coca-Cola together. Thank you for always being a sounding board and for your steadfast encouragement over the years.

And, of course, to the many friends who shared words of support with calls and messages – there are just too many of you to count. If I have failed to mention by name anyone who has made an incredible contribution to my life, it is solely due to my failing memory, not malice. I hope for your understanding and forgiveness.

To my girlfriend, **Ndileka Kalipa**, you have been my pillar of strength in ways I didn't know were possible. You sacrificed time, shared wisdom, and even solved problems I didn't know needed solving – like lending me your dual monitor when my laptop was in a precarious state. What began as a practical fix became an indispensable part of my writing process. Your love and support have been the silent hand guiding me through this journey.

To my long-standing publisher, **Andrea Nattrass**, thank you for believing in my stories and giving them a home across all five of my books. And, of course, to my editor, **Kelly Norwood-Young**, who has edited four of those books – I feel like you know me more than I know myself at this point.

Lastly, to everyone who buys my books, whether you've been with me since the beginning or are discovering my work for the first time, thank you. You are the reason stories like these live beyond the pages. Without readers, stories remain untold and unheard.

This book is as much yours as it is mine.

www.ingramcontent.com/pod-product-compliance
Lightning Source LLC
Chambersburg PA
CBHW011306150426
43191CB00017B/2356